KYUUTO!
JAPANESE CRAFTS!
LACY CROCHET!

Kawaii Resu Ami Zakka
Copyright © 2006 by SHUFU-TO-SEIKATSUSHA

First published in the United States in 2007 by Chronicle
Books LLC.

English translation rights arranged with SHUFU-TO-SEIKAT-
SUSHA, Tokyo through Timo Associates, Inc. Tokyo

Library of Congress Cataloging-in-Publication Data available.

ISBN: 978-0-8118-6058-1

Manufactured in China

Original book design: Hiromi Maruyama
Book design for English edition: Eiko Nishida (cooltiger),
Andrew Pothecary (forbidden colour)
Cover design: River Jukes-Hudson
Photography: Akiko Oshima
Styling: Kumiko Uematsu
Artwork: Mayumi Kawai, Yasuko Sebata, SACHIYO*FUKAO
Texts and template drawings: comomo, So Mochizuki
Technical supervising: Hatoko Sato
English translation: Seishi Maruyama
English copyediting: Alma Reyes-Umemoto (ricorico)
Original book concept: Hanako Hironaka (E&G Creates)
Production assistant: Aki Ueda (ricorico)
Chief editor and production: Rico Komanoya (ricorico)

10 9 8 7 6 5 4 3 2 1

Chronicle Books LLC
680 Second Street
San Francisco, California 94107

www.chroniclebooks.com

Contents

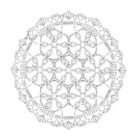

PART 1

Small Crafts for Interiors

Use handmade coasters or covers for your baskets or boxes. Everyday life can be much more fun with these little creations. Why don't you make small items like these for your home?

● Coasters

You only need to crochet about ten rows to make a small coaster. It would be nice to be able to create handy coasters for use at any time. A circle, triangle, or square…which one would you like to make first?

*For method
see pages 40-42*

It's not hot at all!

For method
see page 44

❀ Pot Holders

Popular pot holders are
made in double layers.
First, crochet the front and
the back sides separately
using the same basic
pattern, and then stitch
them together.

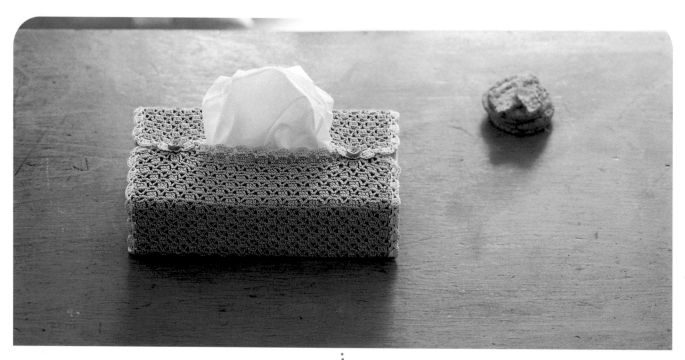

● Tissue Box Cover

It can be a tissue box cover or a place mat. However you choose to use it, it's a chic item with many purposes. Crochet the same two patterns for the upper and lower halves.

Just fold it out easily!

For method
see page 51

◈ Jar Covers

Crochet the round bottom part and then repeat single and double crochets. For a striped pattern, use different colors for certain rows. Match your covers with cups and pretty bottles.

For method see page 53

Baby Shoes 1 (Ties)

These cute baby shoes are so small but stitched with every
detail and care. They are accented by light-blue round edges
and flower motifs at the tips of the laces.

*For method
see page 55*

✿ Baby Shoes 2 (Straps)

These baby boots have straps and decorative orange edges.
The sides are crocheted in the same pattern as Baby Shoes
1 (facing page).

For method
see page 56

Doily 1 (Round)

This doily has a soft and tender design consisting of six large petals stretched all around. If you pass a lace tie through the edge, it can become a fashionable flower pot cover!

For method see page 24

Doily 2 (Square)

A handy square doily is very easy to crochet because it repeats three row patterns. The simple and modest colors stand out beautifully.

For method see page 28

Multipurpose Cover

This cover has many uses, and shows fresh striped patterns with three natural colors. It is fashioned in the same way as the doily above but for about twice its length.

For method see page 58

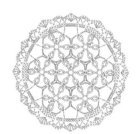

PART 2

Private Time for Favorite Handicrafts

It's always nice to be surrounded by your own handmade items among other hand-crocheted or needlework crafts. While using your handmade pincushion and scissors case (page 14), you find yourself making more crafts, and enjoying each step immensely.

For method see page 43

● Pincushion

A pincushion is a must for making handicrafts. Lay two square patterns together and join them by stitching over the edges.

✿ Lace Basket

Tables tend to look messy with small articles placed randomly on them.
This basket is useful to organize your personal items. It will be firmly shaped
if you crochet it tightly.

*For method
see page 60*

Put your small items in this basket.

● Scissors Case

This case for sewing scissors has a lid flap with cute triangle motifs
(see facing page). Match the color of the felt with the lace thread.

*For method
see page 62*

❀ Hook Case

An original hook case is one item you might wish to have someday. It's easy to make
and can be fashionable if you use a piece of linen for the inner lining (see facing page).

*For method
see page 64*

Braid 1 (Ribbon) • Braid 2 (Edging)

Braid lace can be crocheted like a ribbon and is an effective accent for decoration. Adjust its size to the object you want to decorate.

For method see pages 47-49

[Edging]

[Ribbon]

You can
hide your
clutter inside
these jars!

Braid 3 (Ringlet)

When you use a braid as a bottle or jar jacket, make a ring with it by interweaving
the beginning and the end of the braid. Simple jars look more fashionable.

For method
see page 50

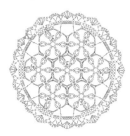

PART 3

Fashionable Items for Everyday Life

Carrying your own handmade items outdoors brings a happy experience.
If someone tells you, "Oh, they're so cute!" you tend to make even more.
Small, stylish lace crochet items are so fun to make!

*For method
see page 70*

● Mobile Phone Case

A mobile phone case can be crocheted with a firm basic
pattern, so your mobile phone is secure in it. It can also be used
as a mini-bag for lipsticks or keys.

Corsage 1 (Gerbera; left) • Corsage 2 (Rose)

A daisy- or rose-shaped corsage looks very chic on your bag, hat, the chest of your sweater, or the collar of your coat. What colors are your favorite for different seasons?

For method
see page 66-68

Potpourri Sachet 1 (Flowers; left) • Potpourri Sachet 2 (Leaves)

Tiny flowers and leaves are used as motifs for these cute sachets. Why don't you put one in your closet or bag, and enjoy its fashionable scent?

For method see pages 72-75

This purse can hold
a lot of coins.

Coin Purse

Crochet in increasing circles from the center to six directions, then stitch the
purse frame. Accentuate the purse with decorative leaves.

For method
see page 68

*Crochet from the bottom in
circles.*

● Decorative Strings 1 (Balls) • Decorative Strings 2 (Tassels)

Bind them around a hat, use as a belt, or hang them casually on the wall as decoration—
everyone can use them in different ways. You can also make one with leftover thread.

*For method
see pages 76-77*

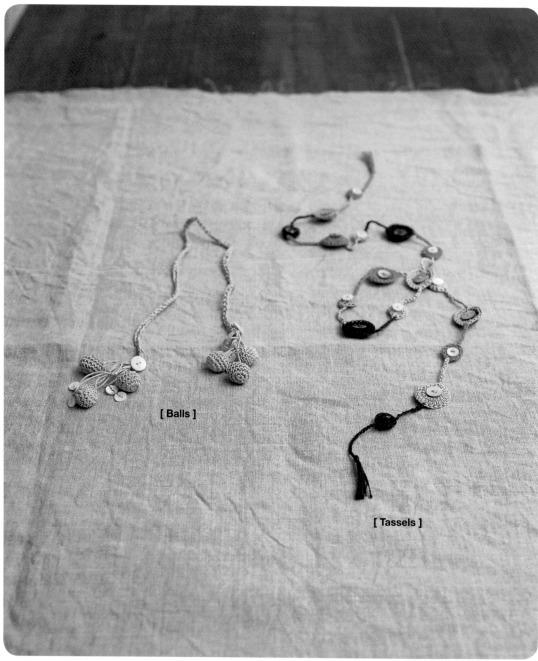

[Balls]

[Tassels]

[Petals]

[Buttons]

Mini Bag 1 (Petals) • Mini Bag 2 (Buttons)

It's a fun idea to redesign your bags or shirts with lace yarn. You can add small flower motifs, buttons, cross stitches, or fringes.

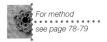

For method
see page 78-79

PATTERN LESSON 1
Crocheting Rings of Circles

● ROUND DOILY
See page 10 for photo

Materials

Light blue doily
Lace thread
Light blue, 0.7 oz (20 g)
Plain cotton thread, 31.5 in (80 cm)
Blue bead, 1 piece

Brown doily
Lace thread
Light brown, 0.7 oz (20 g)

Crochet hook
Size 6
(1.75 mm)

Pattern Size
9.8 in (25 cm) diameter

Crochet Steps

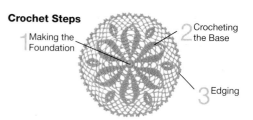

1 Making the Foundation
2 Crocheting the Base
3 Edging

Refer to stitch demos on the following pages to complete this pattern lesson.

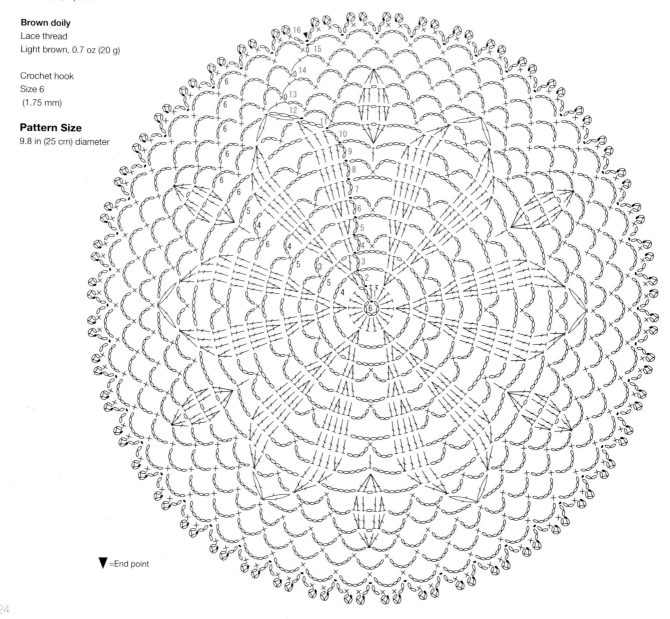

▼ =End point

How to Hold the Thread and the Hook

(See pages 33-39 for more details.)

● How to Pull Out the Thread's End

Peel off the label of the ball of thread and pick out the thread's end from the outer side. Put the ball in a plastic bag to protect it, then secure the bag with a rubber band.

● How to Throw the Thread Over the Left Hand

1 As shown above, pass the thread through the fingers and bring its end to the front.

2 Hold the thread's end gently with the thumb and middle finger, and adjust it with the forefinger.

● How to Hold Hook with the Right Hand

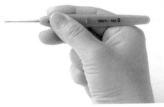

Hold the hook gently with the thumb and forefinger, and support it with the middle finger while crocheting.

Crocheting a Chain of Circle Rings

● How to Make the First Chain

1 Place the hook over the thread from behind, then insert the hook and wind the thread once toward the direction of the arrow as shown above.

2 Hold the thread with the thumb and middle finger, and loop the thread over the hook and draw through.

3 The first chain stitch is now completed, but this chain is *not* counted as one ring.

● How to Make the Chain of Circle Rings

4 Throw the thread over the hook and draw through toward the direction of the arrow as shown above. This is the first chain of the circle ring.

5 For the second chain, loop the thread again over the hook and draw through. Repeat this step four more times.

6 The chains are now completed.

● Drawing Through

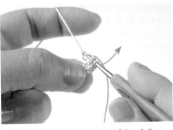

7 To finish the foundation of the doily, insert the hook into the first chain and draw through toward the direction of the arrow as shown above.

8 The base chain of the circle ring is now completed.

First Ring

● Double Crochet

1 Begin with three chains. Throw the thread over the hook, and pick up the entire chain and draw through toward the direction of the arrow as shown above.

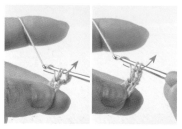

2 Throw the thread over the hook and draw through the two loops together. Again, throw the thread over the hook and draw through the remaining two loops together.

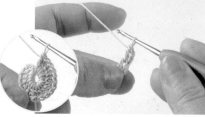

3 A double crochet is completed. Do 16 more double crochet for a total of 18 stitches. (Count the first three chains as one stitch.)

4 To finish the ring, insert the hook into the third chain (top of the chain) and draw through.

2nd to 11th Rings

● Two Double Crochet Increase

1 To do the second ring, begin with three chains, and do a double crochet at the third chain in the previous round.

2 Do a double crochet again in the same chain.

● Three Double Crochet Increase

3 Repeat the following pattern around: four chains, skip the next two stitches, do three double crochets at the third stitch. End with four chains and draw through to finish.

● Single Crochet

4 To do the 4th ring, pick up the entire chain in the previous rounds and do a single crochet.

5 Insert the hook toward the direction of the arrow as shown in the photo in step 4, then pull out the thread and draw through. A single crochet is completed. Work four more rings, following the pattern.

● Two Double Crochet Decrease

Incomplete double crochet stitch

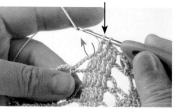

6 To do a two double crochet decrease starting from the 9th ring, throw the thread over the hook leaving an incomplete double crochet on the hook, then insert the hook into the next stitch.

Incomplete double crochet stitch

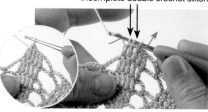

7 Make another incomplete double crochet, and draw through all three loops. A two double crochet decrease is completed. Work another ring of increases, as indicated in the diagrams on page 24.

● Three Double Crochet Decrease

8 To do a three double crochet decrease in the 11th ring, make three incomplete double crochets on the hook and draw through all four loops as illustrated in step 7.

12th to 16th Rings

● Four Double Crochet Cluster Variations

1 To do the first cluster, make one incomplete double crochet at the first three chains and a stitch in the previous round, then make two incomplete double crochets in the next stitch.

2 Throw the thread over the hook and draw through all the four loops toward the direction of the arrow as shown in the right photo in step 1 above. This completes one cluster variation.

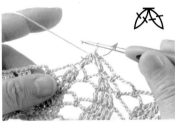

3 To do the second cluster and thereafter, make two incomplete double crochets at each stitch in the previous round, and draw through all five loops.

● 12th to the End of the 14th Ring

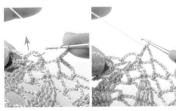

4 Begin with three chains and make a double crochet in the first chain. Work a cluster for the 12th round, a single crochet for the 13th and 14th rings.

● 13th to the Beginning of the 15th Ring

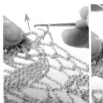 

5 Begin with one chain, and pick up the entire double crochet at the end of the previous round, then do a single crochet.

● Single Crochet with a Picot in the 16th Ring

6 Make two chains and a single crochet, then make three chains and insert the hook into the top of the single crochet and draw through.

7 A single crochet with a picot is completed.

● Drawing Through in the 16th Ring

8 To finish one chain, insert the hook into one of the single crochet loops behind and pull through.

Fastening at the Last Stage

1 To finish the pattern, cut the thread leaving about 6 inches (15 cm) and pull out the last loop.

2 Slip the thread through the sewing needle and insert it toward the back, drawing through the stitches, then cut.

3 To fasten the stitches, draw though a few stitches from the back and cut the thread.

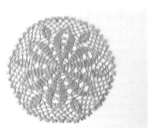

4 The doily is now completed. Steam iron it to adjust its shape.

Crocheting a Flat Pattern from a Chained Cast-on

● SQUARE DOILY

See page 11 for photo

Materials

Lace thread
Ivory, 0.71 oz (20 g)
Light brown or alternate color, 0.35 oz (10 g)

Crochet hook
Size 6 (1.75 mm)

Pattern Size

7.68 in × 10.24 in
(19.5 cm × 26 cm)

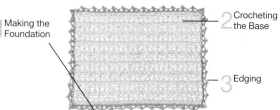

Crochet Steps

1 Making the Foundation

2 Crocheting the Base

3 Edging

—— = Ivory

—— = Light brown

▼ = End point

▽ = Start-off point

Refer to stitch demos on the following pages to complete this pattern lesson.

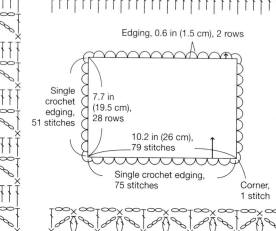

Edging, 0.6 in (1.5 cm), 2 rows

Single crochet edging, 51 stitches

7.7 in (19.5 cm), 28 rows

10.2 in (26 cm), 79 stitches

Single crochet edging, 75 stitches

Corner, 1 stitch

→ ㉘
← ㉗
→ ㉖

← ⑤
→ ④
← ③ ⎫
→ ② ⎬ One repeat pattern
← ① ⎭

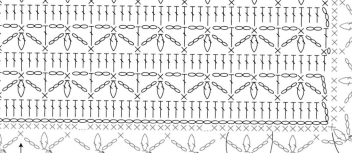

Start-off point

Center

One repeat of a 6-stitch edging

One single crochet at the corner

Crocheting the Base/ Chained Cast-on

(See pages 33-39 for more details.)

1 First, make 79 chains.

Base/1st Row

● **Double Crochet**

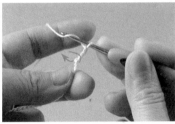

2 Make three chains in the first row. Then, throw the thread over the hook and insert the hook into the rear loop of the 5th chain.

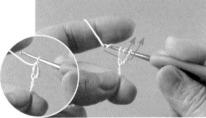

3 Draw through twice toward the direction of the arrow, as shown above, to complete a double crochet.

4 Double crochet across for a total of 79 stitches in the first row. Count the first three chains as one stitch.

Base/2nd Row

● **Preliminary Chains**

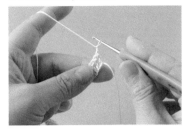

1 Make one chain. Do not count this step as one stitch.

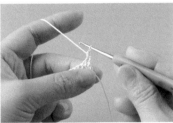
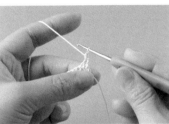

2 Do one single crochet on the first chain in the previous row. Then, make three chains.

● **Two Double-Crochet Clusters**

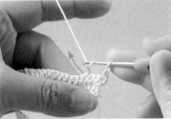
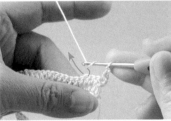

3 Skip two stitches and do a two double-crochet cluster on the next stitch.

Incomplete double crochet stitch

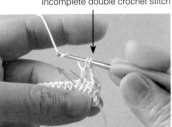

4 Weave one more incomplete double crochet on the same stitch while leaving one incomplete double crochet on the hook.

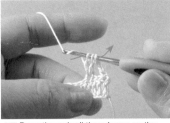

5 Draw through all three loops on the hook.

6 The two double-crochet cluster is now completed.

7 Make three chains and a single crochet on the third stitch from the cluster. This completes the repeat pattern.

● **Last Stitch**

8 Insert the hook into the rear loop and the outer loop of the third preliminary chain in the previous row, then do a single crochet.

29

Base/3rd–28th Row

● 3rd Row

1 Make three chains and repeat the following across: 2 chains, 1 single crochet, 2 chains, 1 double crochet.

5 Repeat the pattern across, alternating between two double crochet picking up the loops in the previous row (Step 3) and a double crochet into a single crochet in the previous row (Step 4).

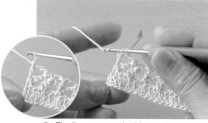

2 Finally, weave a double crochet into the single crochet of the previous row to complete the pattern.

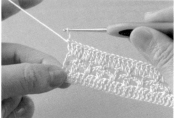

6 Crochet into the three preliminary chains in the previous row to finish the pattern.

● 4th Row

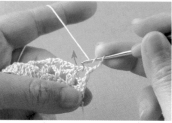

3 Make three chains and pick up the entire loops in the previous row to make two double crochets.

● 5th Row and Onward

7 Sew the 5th through the 28th rows the same way as the 2nd through the 4th rows. Leave 6 inches of the thread's end and pass it through the last stitch.

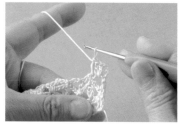

4 Stitch the next double crochet into a single crochet in the previous row.

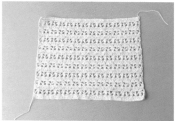

8 The base is now completed. The thread's end comes at the top right side of the base.

Edging in the Alternate Color

● 1st Round

1 Start with a new thread at the second stitch from the right of the 28th row, and make one chain.

2 (Top) Single crochet across, stitching into the double crochets of the upper side of the base. At even intervals, skip four stitches for a total of 75 stitches.

3 (Corner) Weave two stitches into the preliminary chains in the 28th row.

4 (Left side) To edge the left side of the base (stitching into the double crochets), pick up the stitches evenly for a total of 51 stitches (see Symbol Chart on page 39).

● **2nd Round/Cluster with a Picot**

5 Insert the hook through the top edge to do a single crochet.

9 Make one chain, a single crochet, and three chains. Make a two double-crochet cluster to stitch the next cluster with a picot.

1 Cut the thread leaving about 6 inches, and pull the last loop to slip the thread through a darning needle.

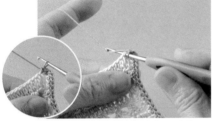

6 (Bottom) Insert the hook through the two loops of the chain, then single crochet across while skipping four stitches.

10 Make 3 chains and insert the hook into the top of the cluster, and draw though.

2 Insert the needle into the single crochet loop in the 2nd round, and pull the needle backward. Pick up the loop of the single crochet in the first round and draw through, then cut the thread.

7 (Right side) Crochet the right side of the base the same way as the left side. Then, draw through the first single crochet to finish the first round.

11 A cluster with a picot is now completed (see Three-Chain Picot page 39).

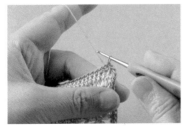

8 The first round of edging is now completed.

12 Continue the picot pattern around.

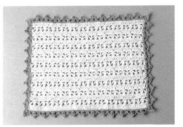

3 Steam iron the doily to adjust its shape.

Lacy Crochet Techniques

The following techniques and charts will help you learn basic to complex crochet stitches so that you can easily follow any crochet pattern. Less experienced crocheters may want to practice by stitching a simple chain (page 35) and trying the various stitches just for fun. When you feel more confident, choose a simple pattern, such as Round Coaster (page 40). Practice training your eye to first skim the pattern diagram and notice how the stitches fit together to form each design—then consult the pattern text for clarification, referring to the techniques section as needed. In no time at all, you will master every stitch and pattern in this book!

How to Thread Over and Hold a Hook

1 Hold the tip of the thread with the right hand. Throw the thread over the left hand from the back through the little finger and the ring finger. Then, thread over the forefinger from the back and pull it forward.

Tip of the thread

2 Hold the tip of the thread with the thumb and the middle finger, and hold up the forefinger to stretch the thread.

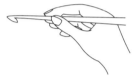

3 Hold the hook gently with the thumb and forefinger, then support its tip with the middle finger.

How to Make the First Stitch

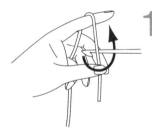

1 Throw the thread over the hook and wind once toward the direction of the arrow as shown in the diagram.

2 The thread should form a loop over the hook.

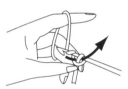

3 Hold the tail of the thread with the thumb and the middle finger as you draw through toward the direction of the arrow.

4 Pull the tip of the thread to tighten it. The first stitch is completed, but is not counted as one stitch.

Making Chain Stitches

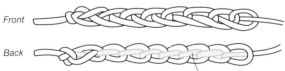

Front

Back

Back loop of the chain

Chain stitches have front and back sides, and the stitch that shows from the back is called a "back loop of the chain." See Chain Stitch on page 35.

Picking up the front loop and back loop of the chain

Picking up only the back loop of the chain

Picking up only the front loop of the chain

These three methods show the different styles of picking up the thread in crocheting the first round or row.

Cast-on Foundation

Crocheting in Circles from the Center (Making a Ring with the Thread's End)

   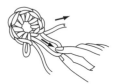

1 Loop the thread twice around the left forefinger.

2 Pull out the ring with the right hand and hold it with the left hand. Insert the hook into the ring and throw the thread over.

3 Draw the thread through, then make a preliminary chain.

4 To do the first round, insert the hook into the center ring and make as many stitches as required.

5 Put down the hook and pull the inner thread in the first round to fasten it, then gently pull the thread's end to fasten.

6 To finish this round, insert the hook into the first stitch. Throw the thread over and draw through.

Crocheting in Circles from the Center (Making a Ring with Chains)

1 Crochet as many chains as required (see Chain Stitch on facing page), and insert the hook into the front loop of the first chain, then draw through.

2 Throw the thread over and make a preliminary chain stitch (or more as required).

3 To do the first round, insert the hook and sew toward the direction of the arrow as shown in the diagram, then draw a bundled loop (see Two Double Crochet Cluster: Picking Up a Bundle on page 39).

4 To finish the first round, insert the hook into the preliminary chain stitch and draw through.

Flat Crocheting

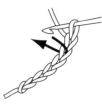  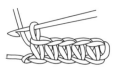

1 Sew the number of chains required plus one preliminary chain, then insert the hook into the front loop and rear loop of the second chain from the hook.

2 Throw the thread over and draw the loop through toward the direction of the arrow as shown in the diagram.

3 Repeat the previous steps to the end of the first round.

Picking Up a Stitch

The method for picking up a stitch for clusters may vary according to the pattern. The symbol with a closed bottom means that the hook is inserted into one stitch in the previous row—also referred to as the two double crochet cluster (dc cl) but weaving into the previous row). The symbol with an open bottom means that the entire chain is picked up or wrapped.

 Weave into one chain in the previous row.

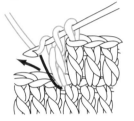 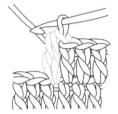

 Pick up the entire chain stitch in the previous row.

Stitch Techniques and Symbols/Abbreviations

Chain Stitch (ch)

1 Thread over and make a first stitch (see page 33. Move the hook toward the direction of the arrow as shown in the diagram, and draw the thread through the loop of the first stitch.

2 Draw through the second stitch the same way as the first one.

3 Repeat for the number of stitches desired.

Slip Stitch (Sl st)

1 Insert the hook into the previous row, and throw the thread over the hook toward the direction of the arrow. as shown in the diagram.

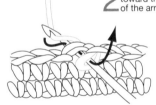

2 Draw the thread toward the direction of the arrow.

3 Draw though to finish with a single loop on the hook.

Using the Symbol/Abbreviation Charts

Symbol/Abbreviation Chart for Crocheting in a Circle from the Center

The design in this crochet pattern is a ring in the center that uses a knitting technique of sewing in a circle in single rounds. Hold the pattern with the front side up, and start sewing the foundation. Then, crochet while reading the symbols from right to left. In the fifth row as shown in the chart, hold the pattern from the reverse side and crochet while reading the symbols from left to right. The symbol △ indicates where to start the new thread, and the symbol ▲ indicates where to cut the thread.

Symbol/Abbreviation Chart for Flat Crochet

In flat crochet, chains run on both right and left sides. When a preliminary chain is placed on the right side, hold the pattern from the front side up and crochet while reading the symbols from right to left. When a preliminary chain is placed on the left side, hold the pattern on the reverse side and crochet while reading the symbols from left to right.

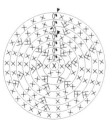

6th-7th row: Crochet from the front side.
5th row: Crochet from the rear side.
1st-4th row: Crochet from the front side.

▼ = End point
▽ = Starting-off point

6th row →
4th row →
2nd row →
← 5th row
← 3rd row
← 1st row

Preliminary chain on the left side, crocheted on the reverse side

Preliminary chain on the right side, crocheted on the front side

Single Crochet (sc)

1 Insert the hook in the previous row, and throw the thread over the hook toward the direction of the arrow as shown in the diagram, then draw the loop through.

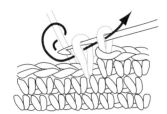

2 Throw the thread over the hook toward the direction of the arrow and draw through two loops together.

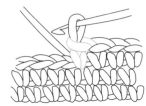

3 This completes a single crochet.

Half Double Crochet (hdc)

1 Throw the thread over the hook, and insert the hook in the previous row toward the direction of the arrow as shown in the diagram. Then, throw the thread again over the hook to draw the loop through.

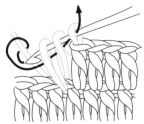

2 Throw the thread over the hook toward the direction of the arrow, and draw through all three loops.

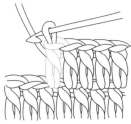

3 This completes a half double crochet.

Double Crochet (dc)

1 Throw the thread over the hook, and insert the hook in the previous row toward the direction of the arrow as shown in the diagram. Then, throw the thread over again to draw the loop through.

2 Throw the thread over the hook toward the direction of the arrow and draw through two loops together. Throw the thread over the hook again and draw through the remaining two loops.

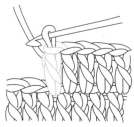

3 This completes a double crochet.

Treble Crochet (tr)

1 Loop the thread twice around the hook, and insert the hook into the previous row toward the direction of the arrow as shown in the diagram. Then, throw the thread again over the hook to draw a loop through.

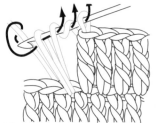

2 Throw the thread over the hook toward the direction of the arrow, and draw through two loops together. Repeat to draw through two loops together. Repeat a third time to draw through the remaining two loops.

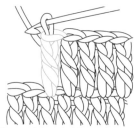

3 This completes a treble crochet.

Reverse Single Crochet (reverse sc)

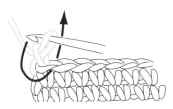  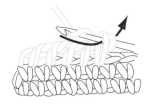

1 Make one preliminary chain (to start a row) and insert the hook into the previous row toward the direction of the arrow as shown in the diagram, while holding the fabric front side up.

2 Throw the thread over the hook and draw the loop through. Throw the thread over the hook again, and draw through two loops together.

3 Insert the hook into the next stitch of the previous row and repeat the same steps, crocheting each stitch from left to right, traveling backward across the row.

Two Single Crochet Increase (sc inc)

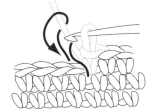 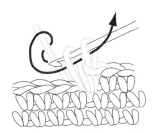 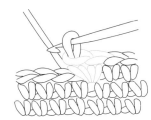

1 Make one single crochet and insert the hook into the same stitch again.

2 Complete a second single crochet.

3 Two single crochets are woven into one stitch and one stitch is increased.

Two Single Crochet Decrease (sc dec)

  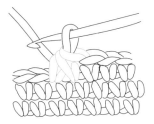

1 Make incomplete single crochets in two stitches in the previous row (see Single Crochet Step 1 on facing page).

2 Throw the thread over the hook toward the direction of the arrow, and draw through all the three loops.

3 This completes a two single crochet decrease, and one stitch is decreased.

Two Half-Double Crochet Increase (hdc inc)

  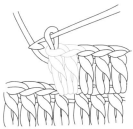

1 Make one half-double crochet, and throw the thread over the hook. Insert the hook into the same stitch toward the direction of the arrow, and draw a loop through.

2 Throw the thread over the hook toward the direction of the arrow and draw through all the three loops.

3 Two half-double crochets are woven into one stitch, and one stitch is increased.

Two Half-Double Crochet Decrease (hdc dec)

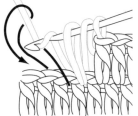

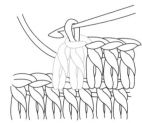

1 Make incomplete half-double crochets in two stitches in the previous row (see Half Double Crochet Step 1 on page 36).

2 Throw the thread over the hook toward the direction of the arrow, and draw through all five loops.

3 This completes a two half-double crochet decrease, and one stitch is decreased.

Two Double Crochet Increase (dc inc)

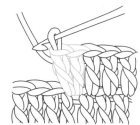

1 Make one double crochet, and throw the thread over the hook. Insert the hook into the same stitch toward the direction of the arrow, and draw a loop through.

2 Throw the thread over the hook toward the direction of the arrow, and draw through the two loops. Throw the thread over the hook again and draw through the remaining two loops.

3 Two double crochets are woven into one stitch, and one stitch is increased.

Two Double Crochet Decrease (dc dec)

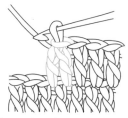

1 Make incomplete double crochets in two stitches in the previous row to end with three loops on the hook (see Double Crochet Steps 1 and 2 on page 36).

2 Throw the thread over the hook toward the direction of the arrow, and draw through the three loops.

3 This completes the two double crochet decrease, and one stitch is decreased.

Three Half-Double Crochet Cluster (hdc cl)

1 Make three incomplete half-double crochets in one stitch in the previous row (see Half Double Crochet Step 1 on page 36).

2 Throw the thread over the hook toward the direction of the arrow, and draw through all seven loops.

3 This completes a three half-double crochet cluster.

Two Double Crochet Cluster (dc cl)
(Weaving into the Previous Row)

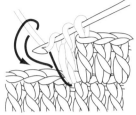

1 Make two incomplete double crochets in one stitch in the previous row to end with three loops on the hook (see Double Crochet Steps 1 and 2 on page 36).

2 Throw the thread over the hook toward the direction of the arrow, and draw through all three loops.

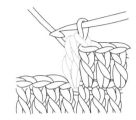

3 This completes a two double crochet cluster.

Two Double Crochet Cluster (dc cl)
(Picking Up a Bundle)

1 Pick up a bundle of chains, and make two incomplete double crochets to end with three loops on the hook (see Double Crochet Steps 1 and 2 on page 36).

2 Throw the thread over the hook toward the direction of the arrow, and draw through all three loops.

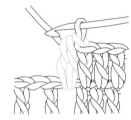

3 This completes a two double crochet cluster picking up a bundle.

Chain Picot (ch p)

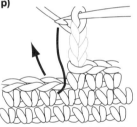

1 Make three (or as called for by the pattern) chain stitches and throw the thread over the hook toward the direction of the arrow as shown in the diagram. Throw the thread over the hook again and draw a loop through.

2 Throw the thread over the hook and draw though toward the direction of the arrow.

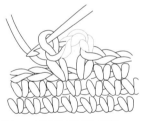

3 This completes a three-chain picot.

Three-Chain Slip Stitch Picot (ch SL sl p)

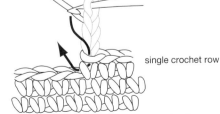

single crochet row

1 Make three chain stitches and insert the hook into the front loop of the top single crochet and the loop on the base toward the direction of the arrow.

2 Throw the thread over the hook, and draw through all the three loops.

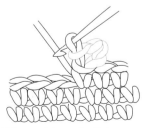

3 This completes a slip stitch picot.

● ROUND COASTER

See page 4 for photo; see Lacy Crochet Techniques (page 33) for stitch guide and illustrated instructions.

. . . .

Materials

Lace thread
Ivory, 0.2 oz (5 g)
Brown, 0.1 oz (2 g)

Crochet hook
Size 4 (2 mm)

Pattern Size

4.5 in (11.5 cm) diameter

Crochet Steps

1 Casting On
Make a cast-on ring (see Crocheting in Circles from the Center: Thread's End, on page 34), then do eight single crochets in the center ring.

2 Crocheting the Base
2nd round: Make three foundation chains. Work double crochet increase around, for a total of 16 stitches, counting the foundation chains. 3rd to 6th rounds: Pick up the bundle of chains in the previous round and make double crochet clusters. For the 7th row, work clusters of 3 double crochets as done previously.

3 Edging
8th round: Pick up the bundle of chains in the previous round, then work a two-double crochet decrease and a five-chain picot while drawing through at the third chain.

Step-by-Step Method

1 Casting On

2 Crocheting the Base

3 Edging

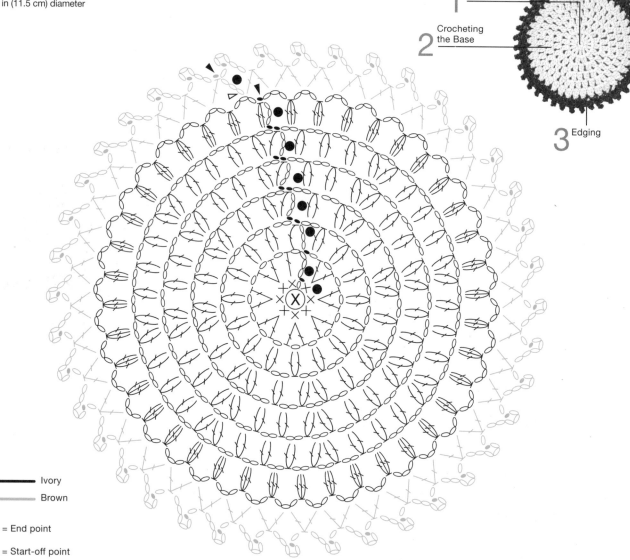

— Ivory

— Brown

▼ = End point

▽ = Start-off point

40

● TRIANGLE COASTER

See page 4 for photo; see Lacy Crochet Techniques (page 33) for stitch guide and illustrated instructions.

Materials

Lace thread
Ivory, 0.1 oz (3 g)
Green, 0.1 oz (2 g)
Light brown, 0.05 oz (1 g)

Crochet hook
Size 4 (2 mm)

Pattern Size

H 4.7 in (12 cm)

Tip

It is easier to change threads when knitting the last slip stitch of each round.

— Green

— Light brown

— Ivory

Crochet Steps

1 Casting On

Make a cast-on ring (see Crocheting in Circles from the Center: Thread's End, on page 34), then do six single crochets in the center ring.

2 Crocheting the Base

2nd round: Make three foundation chains and alternate three double crochet clusters and three chains, counting the foundation chain as the first double crochet. 3rd round: Make one chain, single crochet, and make four chains. Skip a chain from the previous round, single crochet, make three chains weaving into the chains of previous round, then single crochet. Repeat around, adding two more four-chain corners. 4th round and onward: Pick up the bundle of chains in the previous round at three corners, double crochet and chain four to make the points (triangle corners). 5th round: Starting from a foundation chain, work double crochet, chain, single crochet pattern along the sides; repeat double crochet and chain four pattern at the three points. 6th to 9th rounds: Alternate foundation chains and single crochet across the sides as shown below; repeat double crochet and chain four pattern at the three points. Finally, pick up the bundle of the first chain and draw through to complete the base of the coaster.

3 Edging

10th round: Make one foundation chain, and pick up the bundle of chains in the previous round to make a single crochet and a chain. Stitch three chain picots on the three double-crocheted corners.

Step-by-Step Method

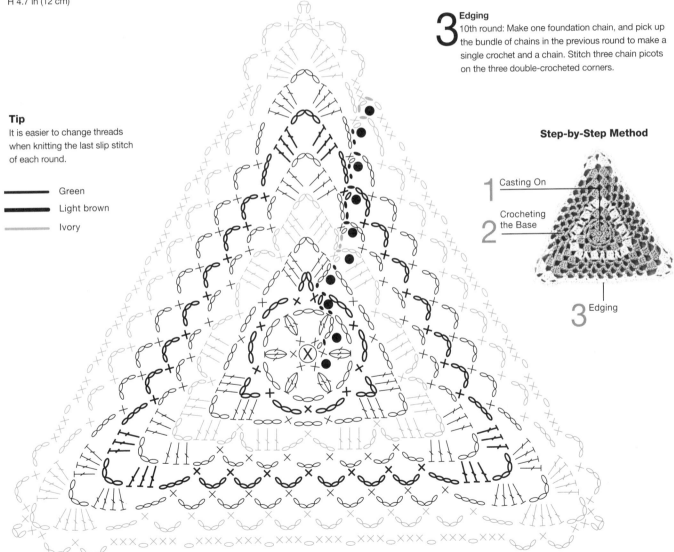

1 Casting On

2 Crocheting the Base

3 Edging

● SQUARE COASTER

See page 4 for photo; see Lacy Crochet Techniques (page 33) for stitch guide and illustrated instructions.

Materials

Lace thread
Light blue, 0.1 oz (3 g)
Ivory, 0.1 oz (3 g)

Crochet hook
Size 4 (2 mm)

Pattern Size

4 in square (10.2 cm square), without picots
4.1 in square (10.5 cm square), with picots

Crochet Steps

1 Casting On

Make a cast-on ring in three chains (see Crocheting in Circles from the Center: Chains, on page 34). Make three foundation chains and repeat five chains and one double crochet around.

2 Crocheting the Base

2nd to 8th rounds: Make three foundation chains—four chains for each corner. Pick up the bundle of chains in the previous round and work in double crochet as illustrated below.

3 Edging

9th round: To sew without picots, use light blue until the 9th round. To sew with picots, change thread to ivory in the 9th round and work in the same way as the pattern without picots. 10th round: Repeat two chains and one slip stitch on the chains in the previous round. To make the corners, make a 3-chain stitch and 5-chain picots.

Tip

It is easier to change threads when knitting the last slip stitch of each round.

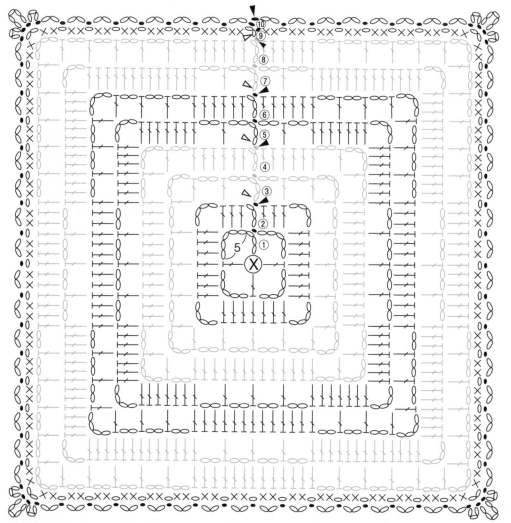

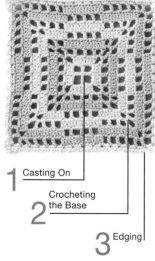

Step-by-Step Method

1 Casting On

2 Crocheting the Base

3 Edging

——— Ivory

——— Light blue

▼ = End point

▽ = Start-off point

● PINCUSHION

See page 12 for photo; see Lacy Crochet Techniques (page 33) for stitch guide and illustrated instructions.

. . . .

Materials

For blue pincushion
Lace thread
Blue, 0.1 oz (4 g)
Light brown, 0.05 oz (1 g)

For pink pincushion
Lace thread
Pink, 0.2 oz (5 g)
1 round button, 0.5 in (1.2 cm)

For both pincushions
Hemp fabric, 2.6 in x 4.5 in (6.5 cm × 11.5 cm)
Cotton stuffing

Crochet hook
Size 4 (2 mm)

Pattern Size

2.3 in square (5.8 cm square)

Crochet Steps

1 Making the Cushion
Leave a seam allowance of 0.3 inch (0.7 cm) and 1 inch (2.5 cm) opening for turning the lining right side out. Stitch the lining with a sewing machine or by hand; turn the cushion right side out and stuff it with cotton, then sew and close the opening.

2 Casting On
Make a cast-on ring in three chains (see Crocheting in Circles from the Center: Chains, on page 34). Repeat four double crochets and three chains alternately, counting the foundation chain as one stitch. To do the last stitch, make one chain and do a half double crochet on the foundation chain.

3 Crocheting the Base
To do the 2nd to 4th rounds, do four double crochets and three chains at the corners, and repeat one double crochet and two chains alternately along the sides. For the blue pincushion, cut the thread at the end of the 4th round and stitch the edges of the 5th round with the alternate color. Repeat the steps to make a second base.

4 Edging
Overlay the pair of base patterns with lining in place and stitch their edges while stuffing the cushion. Sew a button in the center of the pink cushion.

Start-off point for the blue pincushion

——— Light brown edging for blue pincushion

▼ = End point

▽ = Start-off point

Step-by-Step Method

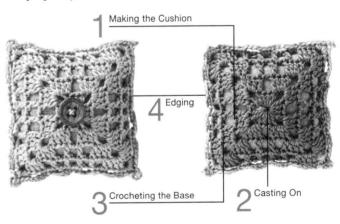

1 Making the Cushion

4 Edging

3 Crocheting the Base

2 Casting On

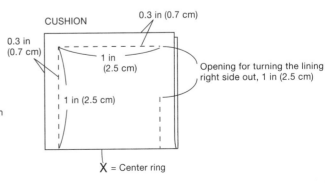

CUSHION

0.3 in (0.7 cm)

0.3 in (0.7 cm)

1 in (2.5 cm)

1 in (2.5 cm)

Opening for turning the lining right side out, 1 in (2.5 cm)

X = Center ring

43

● POT HOLDERS

See page 5 for photo; see Lacy Crochet Techniques (page 33) for stitch guide and illustrated instructions.

· · · · · · · · · · · · · · · · · · · ·

Materials

For orange pot holder
Lace thread
Ivory, 0.7 oz (20 g)
Orange, 0.2 oz (5 g)

For purple pot holder
Lace thread
Ivory, 0.7 oz (20 g)
Purple, 0.1 oz (3 g)
Light brown, 0.1 oz (2 g)
1 round button, 0.5 in (1.3 cm) diameter

Crochet hook
Size 4 (2 mm)

Pattern Size

Approx. 5.9 in (15 cm) diameter

Crochet Steps

1 Casting On
Make a cast-on ring (see Crocheting in Circles from the Center: Chains, on page 34). Make three foundation chains, and then do 17 double crochets into the ring.

2 Crocheting the Base
Rounds 2 to 10: Stretch the circle working in double crochet, single crochet, and chains as shown in the diagram on the facing page. 11th round: Work two-treble crochet decrease and three-treble decreases around. When the 11th round is completed, cut the thread. Repeat the steps to make one more base.

3 Edging
Overlay the pair of base patterns, and stitch the edges working in crochet, single crochet, and chains.

4 Making the Handle
Continue from the edges, and make 20 chains. Draw through on the foundation chain of edges, and do a single crochet of 24 stitches into 20 chains. Draw through again on the foundation chain of edges.

5 Making the Center Decoration
Pick up the double crochets in the third row (front side) and create the central motif as directed on page 46.

6 Finishing Off
Sew the button on the base of the handle.

● Edging

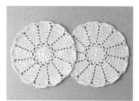

1 Work on the two bases.

2 Overlay the pair back side up, tie the colored thread to the top of a single crochet, then make four chains.

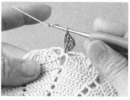

3 Do three treble crochets in the same stitch.

4 When doing a treble crochet and a single crochet, pick up the loops from both bases and sew as shown in the diagram on the facing page.

5 Do a slip stitch on the preliminary chain and continue to stitch the handle to finish the pattern.

Step-by-Step Method

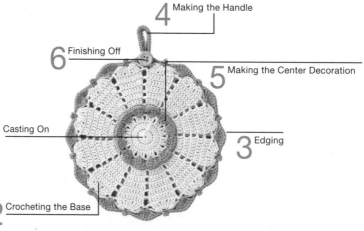

4 Making the Handle
6 Finishing Off
5 Making the Center Decoration
1 Casting On
3 Edging
2 Crocheting the Base

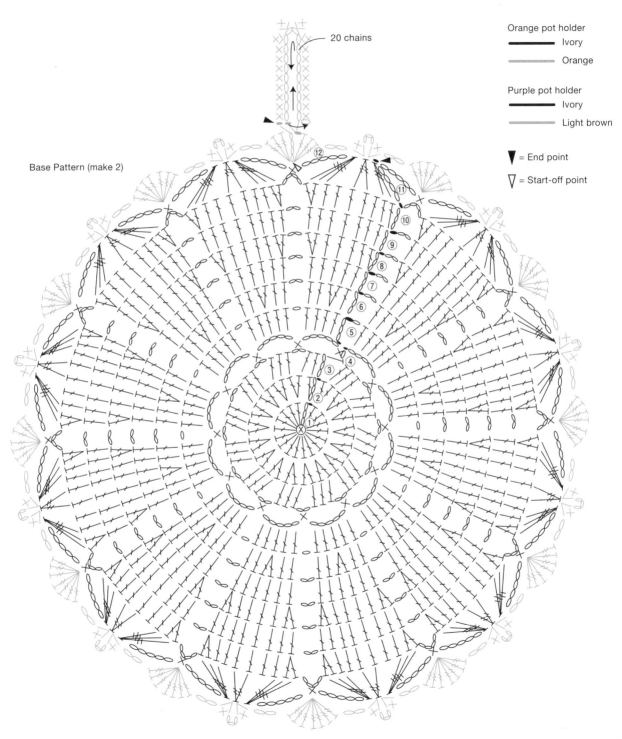

20 chains

Base Pattern (make 2)

● Making the Center Decoration

4th round of the base

Orange pot holder
━━━━━ Orange

Purple pot holder
━━━━━ Purple

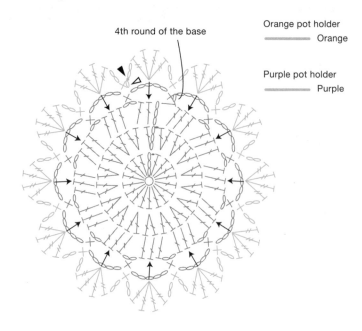

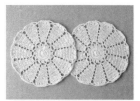

1 Bend the 4th round over, and tie the thread to a single crochet in the 4th round of both bases. Then, make one chain and one single crochet.

2 Make two chains, and pick up the double crochet in the 3rd round of the front side, then do a treble crochet to start the motif design (see Step 3).

3 Do four treble crochets of four stitches into the same stitch, then make two chains.

4 Repeat the motif pattern around (12 repeats in one round).

Finish

Sew the buttons with orange and purple threads respectively.

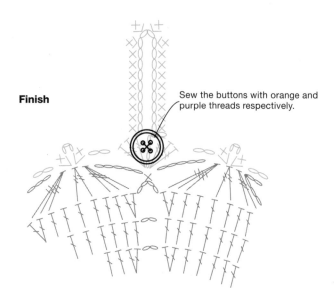

● BRAID 1: RIBBON

See page 16 for photo; see Lacy Crochet Techniques (page 33) for stitch guide and illustrated instructions.
. . . .

Materials

Lace thread
Ivory, 0.92 oz (26 g)

Crochet hook
Size 6 (1.75 mm)

Pattern Size

33.5 in × 2.8 in (85 cm × 7 cm), approx. 1.3 in (3.2 cm) per repeat

Crochet Steps

1 Making the Foundation
Cast-on and make 137 chains.

2 Crocheting the Upper Side of the Base
1st row: Continue making three chains from the cast-on stitch, pick up the rear loop, and insert the hook between the threads to make two double crochets. 2nd to 4th rows: Work double crochet pattern across as shown below. Pick up a bundle of chains in the previous row for the double crochets.

3 Crocheting the Lower Side of the Base
Tie the thread to the preliminary chain, and pick up two cast-on chains to stitch the first row. To do the 1st to the 4th row, stitch in the same way as the upper side.

4 Edging
Stitch the edges to finish.

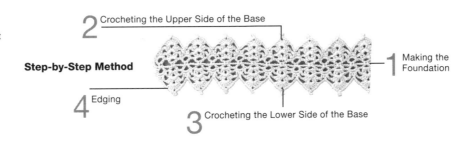

Step-by-Step Method

2 Crocheting the Upper Side of the Base

1 Making the Foundation

4 Edging

3 Crocheting the Lower Side of the Base

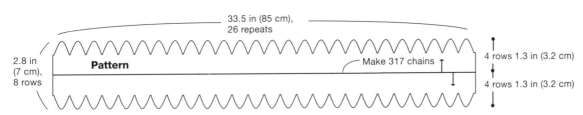

33.5 in (85 cm), 26 repeats

2.8 in (7 cm), 8 rows

Pattern

Make 317 chains

4 rows 1.3 in (3.2 cm)

4 rows 1.3 in (3.2 cm)

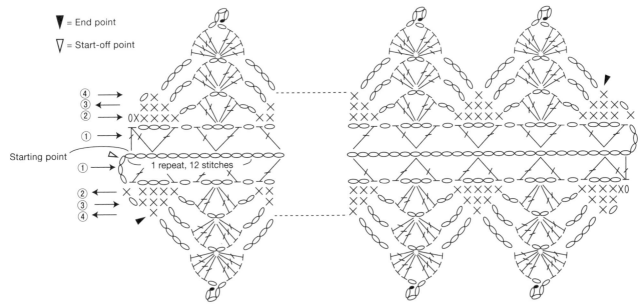

▼ = End point

▽ = Start-off point

④ ③ ②
①

Starting point

①

1 repeat, 12 stitches

② ③ ④

● BRAID 2: EDGING

See page 16 for photo; see Lacy Crochet Techniques (page 33) for stitch guide and illustrated instructions.

. . . .

Materials

Lace thread
Ivory, 1.02 oz (29 g)
Fabric piece, 17.9 in × 13 in (45.5 cm × 32.5 cm)

Crochet hook
Size 4 (2 mm)
Sewing needle and thread

Pattern Size

Width: 1.6 in (4 cm)

Crochet Steps

1 **Making the Foundation**
Cast-on and make 542 chains and draw through the first chain as shown on the diagram on the facing page.

2 **Crocheting the Base**
1st row: Make three foundation chains. Work the 9-stitch double crochet and chain repeat around, stitching into the back loop of the chain. 2nd row: Work the 4-double crochet decrease and 2-double crochet increase around. Make two chains at the corners. 3rd and 4th rows: Pick up a bundle of chains in the previous rows and work the double crochet pattern around. Work chains and single crochets for the 5th row.

3 **Finishing Off**
Place the braid on the fabric and whipstitch it in place, sewing both the front and back sides.

Step-by-Step Method

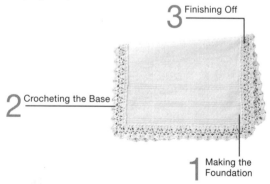

3 Finishing Off

2 Crocheting the Base

1 Making the Foundation

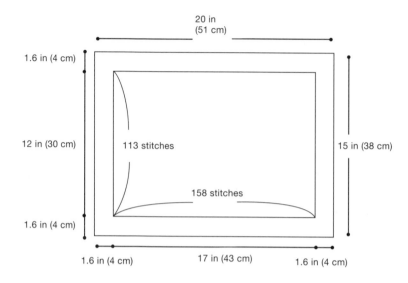

20 in (51 cm)

1.6 in (4 cm)

12 in (30 cm)

15 in (38 cm)

113 stitches

158 stitches

1.6 in (4 cm)

1.6 in (4 cm)   17 in (43 cm)   1.6 in (4 cm)

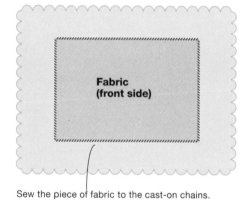

Fabric (front side)

Sew the piece of fabric to the cast-on chains.

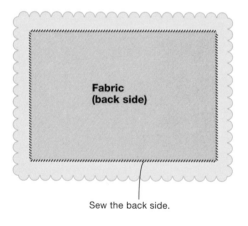

Fabric (back side)

Sew the back side.

48

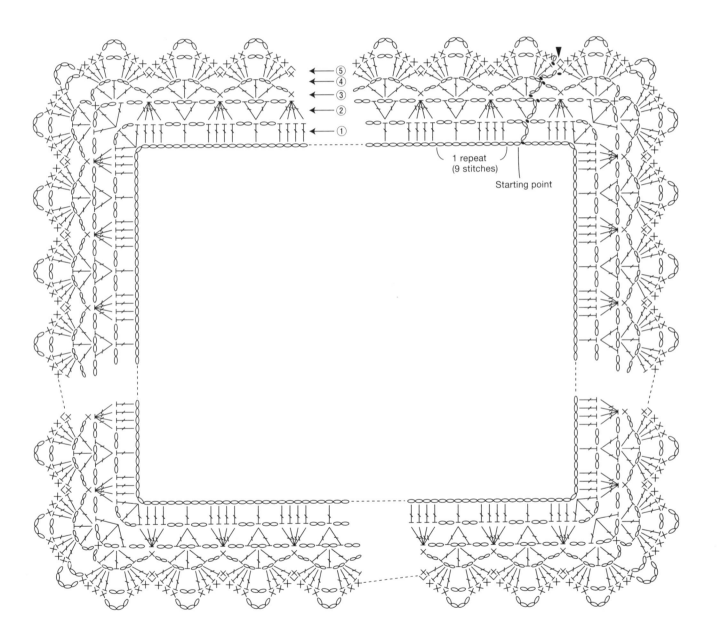

▼ = End point

⑤
④
③
②
①

1 repeat
(9 stitches)

Starting point

● BRAID 3: RINGLET

See page 17 for photo; see Lacy Crochet Techniques (page 33) for stitch guide and illustrated instructions.
. . . .
Materials

Green braid
Lace thread
Green or light blue, 0.5 oz (15 g)

Crochet hook
Size 6 (1.75 mm)

Pattern Size

Approx. 3.2 in × 13 in (8 cm × 32 cm)

Crochet Steps

1 Making the Foundation
Cast-on and make 22 chains.

4 Edging
Crochet the sides of the base as shown in the diagram below. Do a single crochet, double crochet, and treble crochet into the third foundation chain and the top of the double crochet. To finish, draw through the first single crochet.

2 Crocheting the Base
Make three foundation chains continuing from the cast-on chains. Work the flat crochet (see page 39) until the 40th row with double crochets and chains. Cut the thread, leaving a long piece to use for sewing.

3 Forming the Ring
Darn the top and bottom of the base with the long thread's end to make a circle.

4 Edging

Step-by-Step Method

1 Making the Foundation

3 Forming the Ring

2 Crocheting the Base

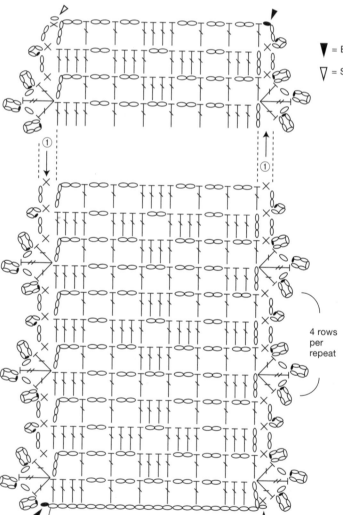

▼ = End point

▽ = Start-off point

① ①

4 rows per repeat

▼ Starting point

Edging
.50 in (1.25 cm), 1 row

13 in (32 cm), 40 rows

2.2 in (5.5 cm), 22 chains

Roll and darn the top and bottom of the base piece.

● TISSUE BOX COVER

See page 6 for photo; see Lacy Crochet Techniques (page 33) for stitch guide and illustrated instructions.

Materials

Lace thread
Green, 1.5 oz (43 g)
Ivory, 0.2 oz (6 g)
Two 0.5 in (1.3 cm) square-faced round buttons

Crochet hook
Size 4 (2 mm)
Sewing needle and thread

Pattern Size

13.8 in × 10.2 in (35 cm × 26 cm)
for a 4.5 in x 10 in x 2 in (11.5 cm × 24 cm × 5 cm) tissue box

Crochet Steps

1 Making the Foundation

Cast-on and make 101 chains.

3 Crocheting the Lower Side of the Base

Tie on, and starting with a net crochet row, repeat the alternating pattern from Step 2 to make a total of 36 rows, ending with a double crochet row. Pull through and cut the thread.

2 Crocheting the Upper Side of the Base

1st row: Make five chains continuing from the cast-on stitch. Pick up the front loop and the rear loop of the cast-on chains and work a single crochet, chain, double crochet pattern across as shown on the diagram on page 52. 2nd row: Pick up a bundle of chains in the previous row and work a net crochet with three chains. Repeat, alternating the two rows to work a total of 35 rows, ending on a double crochet row. Pull through and cut the thread.

4 Edging

Tie the thread to the foundation chain of the last row of the upper side of the base, and make a foundation chain, one single crochet, and three chains in order to do a net crochet. Pick up the loops from the stitch or the row to do the single crochets. To finish the first round, draw through the chain of single crochets and do a net crochet. Work on the same direction for the 2nd round, and draw through the last stitch of the previous row to complete the edges. Tie off.

5 Finishing Off

Place and sew the buttons.

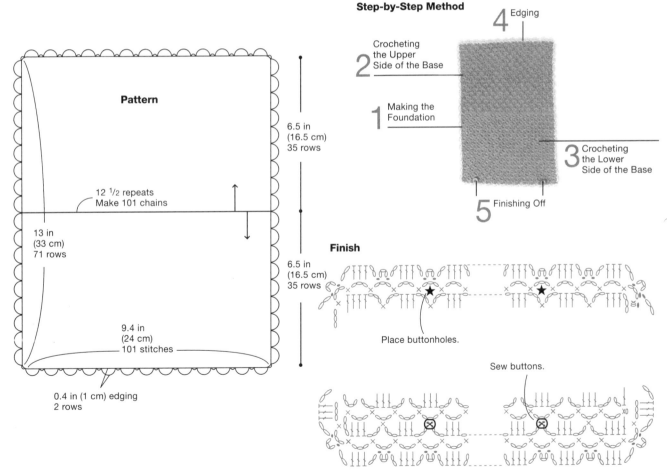

Pattern

12 ¹⁄₂ repeats
Make 101 chains

13 in
(33 cm)
71 rows

9.4 in
(24 cm)
101 stitches

0.4 in (1 cm) edging
2 rows

6.5 in
(16.5 cm)
35 rows

6.5 in
(16.5 cm)
35 rows

Step-by-Step Method

4 Edging

2 Crocheting the Upper Side of the Base

1 Making the Foundation

3 Crocheting the Lower Side of the Base

5 Finishing Off

Finish

Place buttonholes.

Sew buttons.

Pattern for Tissue Box Cover

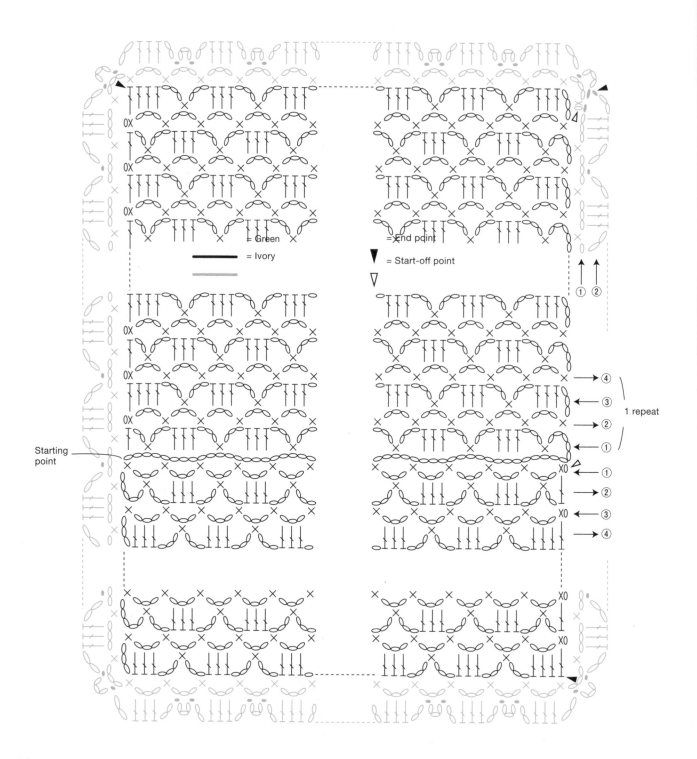

= Green

——— = Ivory

———

= End point

▼ = Start-off point

▽

① ②

→ ④
← ③
→ ②
← ①

1 repeat

▽
← ①
→ ②
← ③
→ ④

Starting point

0X

0X

0X

0X

0X

0X

X0

X0

X0

X0

● JAR COVERS

See page 7 for photo; see Lacy Crochet Techniques (page 33) for stitch guide and illustrated instructions.

Materials

Green jar cover

Lace thread
Ivory, 0.3 oz (8 g)
Green, 0.2 oz (6 g)
One 0.7 in (1.8 cm) square-faced round button

Light blue jar cover

Lace thread
Light blue, 0.3 oz (8 g)
Light brown, 0.2 oz (6 g)
One 0.6 in (1.5 cm) square-faced round button

Orange jar cover

Lace thread
Ivory, 0.3 oz (9 g)
Orange, 0.2 oz (5 g)
Three 0.4 in (1.1 cm) round buttons

Crochet hook
Size 4 (2 mm)
Sewing needle

Pattern Size

Bottom: 2.2 in (5.5 cm) diameter
Height: 2.4 in (6.2 cm)

Crochet Steps

1 Making the Foundation
Make a cast-on ring and one foundation chain. Do ten single crochets into the ring (see Crocheting in Circles from the Center: Thread's End, on page 34).

2 Sewing the Bottom Piece
2nd and 3rd rounds: Weave a double crochet increase into the stitch in the previous row. 4th and 5th rounds: Stretch the pattern by increases as shown in the diagram on page 54. When the 5th row is finished, steam iron the piece to adjust its shape.

3 Crocheting the Side Piece
Continue from the bottom piece to the side section by making a foundation chain. Work in double crochet for the first two rows and crochet until the 15th row without increasing. Change threads according to the applicable color table on page 54.

4 Finishing Off
Sew on the buttons with coordinating color threads.

● Changing Thread Color
(example: orange jar cover)

1 While doing the last double crochet in the 2nd row of the side, draw through with the color thread to finish the stitch.

2 While drawing through the last stitch at the 2nd row, insert the hook into the foundation chain and draw through the color thread.

3 Make one foundation chain and do a single crochet into each stitch.

4 To do the final single crochet, pick up the base yarn, thread over, and draw through.

5 Weave the foundation chain with the base yarn, and do a double crochet in one round.

6 Trail both the base thread and color thread on the reverse side as shown in the photo, and continue sewing.

Step-by-Step Method

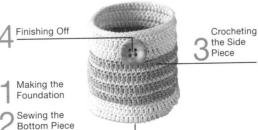

4 Finishing Off

1 Making the Foundation

2 Sewing the Bottom Piece

3 Crocheting the Side Piece

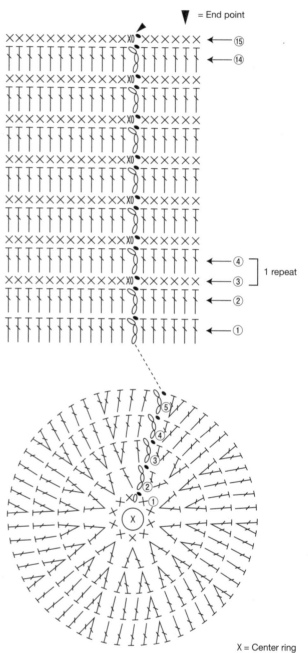

= End point

X = Center ring

1 repeat

● Color Table for Green Jar Cover

Row	Thread Color
11th–15th Row	Ivory
5th–10th Row	Single crochet: Ivory/Double crochet: Green
4th Row	Green
Bottom side, 2 rows of double crochet, 1 row of single crochet	Ivory

● Color Table for Light Blue Jar Cover

Row	Thread Color
15th Row	Light brown
12th–14th Row	Light blue
11th Row	Light brown
8th–10th Row	Light blue
7th Row	Light brown
4th–6th Row	Light blue
Bottom side, 2 rows of double crochet, 1 row of single crochet	Light brown

● Color Table for Orange Jar Cover

Row	Thread Color
5th–15th Row	Single crochet: Orange/Double crochet: Ivory
4th Row	Ivory
3rd Row	Orange
Bottom side, 2 rows of double crochet	Ivory

● Number of Bottom Stitches and Increase

Row	Stitches	Increase
5th Row	60 Stitches	+ 10 stitches
4th Row	50 Stitches	+ 10 stitches
3rd Row	40 Stitches	+ 20 stitches
2nd Row	20 Stitches	+ 10 stitches
1st Row	10 Stitches	

● Finish

Green Jar Cover

Sew the button using the green thread.

11th row

Orange Jar Cover

Sew buttons using the ivory thread.

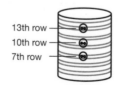

13th row
10th row
7th row

Light Blue Jar Cover

Sew the button using the light blue thread.

11th row

54

● BABY SHOES 1

See page 8 for photo; see Lacy Crochet Techniques (page 33) for stitch guide and illustrated instructions.

Materials

Lace thread
Ivory, 0.5 oz (15 g)
Light blue, 0.4 oz (10 g)
Two 0.4 in (1 cm) shell buttons

Crochet hook
Size 6 (1.75 mm)

Pattern Size

Sole: 3.9 in × 2.4 in (10 cm × 6 cm)
Height: 1.8 in (4.5 cm)

Crochet Steps

1 **Making the Sole**
Instructions for the sole are the same as those for Baby Shoes 2. See page 56 for the pattern.

2 **Making the Sides**
Make 82 chains, and slip stitch to form a loop. Work 8 rows in half double crochet and single crochet as indicated on the diagram below. At the end of each row, turn the work to stitch both the front and reverse sides.

3 **Edging**
Continue from the top of the sides and make 18 repeats of: 1 slip stitch, 3 chains, 1 three-half double crochet cluster.

4 **Making the Shoelace Trimmings**
Make a cast-on ring. Make four chains and stitch a two-double crochet cluster into the first chain. Stitch three chains, one double crochet, three chains, then again draw through the first chain. Repeat to make 3 more sections of the motif. Then, make 60 chains. Do a single crochet into the top center (for the heels). Then, make 60 more chains and stitch the second motif.

5 **Finishing Off**
Place the sole and reverse sides together. Hold the reverse sides in front, and do single crochet stitches with the light blue thread to darn them together (87 stitches). Sew the button on the center of the instep at the 8th row of the sides.

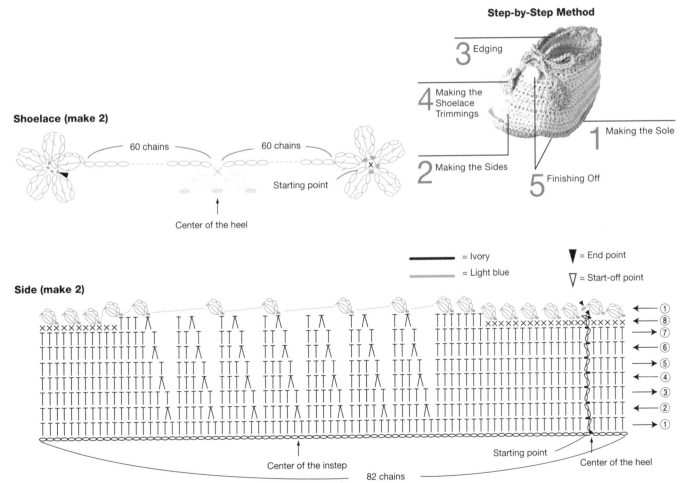

Step-by-Step Method

3 Edging
4 Making the Shoelace Trimmings
1 Making the Sole
2 Making the Sides
5 Finishing Off

Shoelace (make 2)

60 chains — 60 chains

Starting point

Center of the heel

= Ivory
= Light blue
▼ = End point
▽ = Start-off point

Side (make 2)

① ⑧ ⑦ ⑥ ⑤ ④ ③ ② ①

Starting point
Center of the heel
Center of the instep
82 chains

● BABY SHOES 2

See page 9 for photo; see Lacy Crochet Techniques (page 33) for stitch guide and illustrated instructions.

. . . .

Materials

Lace thread
Ivory, 0.6 oz (18 g)
Orange, 0.4 oz (10 g)
Two 0.4 in (1 cm) covered buttons

Crochet hook
Size 6 (1.8 mm)

Pattern Size

Sole: 3.9 in × 2.4 in (10 cm × 6 cm)
Height: 2.6 in (6.5 cm)

Crochet Steps

1 Making the Sole
Make 16 chains and work 6 rows of single crochets and half double crochets, on both sides of the chains as shown in the diagram below. Work the decrease around the toe section.

2 Making the Sides
Make 82 chains, and slip stitch to form a loop. Work 6 rows in half double crochet as indicated on the diagram on the facing page. At the end of each row, turn the work to stitch both the front and reverse sides. 7th to 12th rows: Work a decrease in flat knit as shown in the diagram.

3 Edging
Work one row single crochet for the top of the sides, then repeat three chains and one slip stitch for the ruffle, as indicated on the diagram on the facing page.

4 Making the Covered Button
Make a cast-on ring and one foundation chain, then work a single crochet pattern as indicated on the diagram on the facing page, increasing 6 stitches on the second round for a total of 12 stitches on the last round. Place the button inside after the 3rd round. Sew the 4th row and squeeze.

5 Sewing the Strap
Make 12 chains. Continue, making 5 slip stitches and 6 chains. Do a slip stitch into the first chain, and continue, making 29 chains. Make one foundation chain and work a single crochet for two rows on both sides of the chains. Work running stitches with orange thread doubled for the edge of the strap.

6 Finishing Off
Sew the covered button and the strap to the side piece. Place the sole and reverse sides together. Hold the side in front, and do single crochet stitches using the orange thread to darn them together (87 stitches).

Sole (make 2)

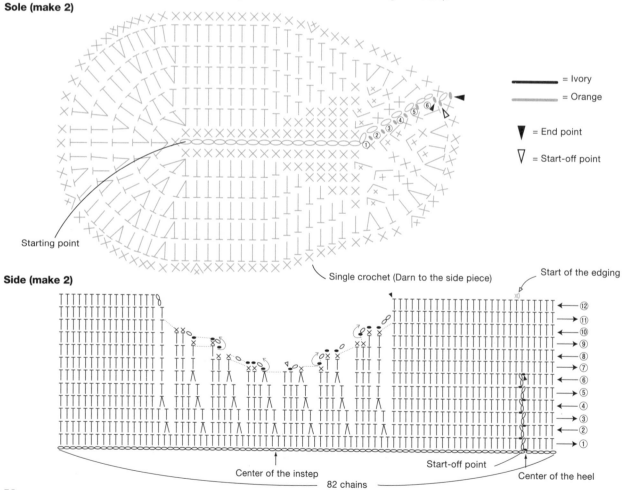

Starting point

= Ivory
= Orange

▼ = End point
▽ = Start-off point

Single crochet (Darn to the side piece)

Start of the edging

Side (make 2)

⑫ ⑪ ⑩ ⑨ ⑧ ⑦ ⑥ ⑤ ④ ③ ② ①

Center of the instep

Start-off point

Center of the heel

82 chains

Edging

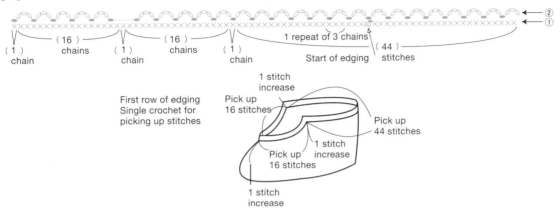

(2)
(1)

(16)
chains

(16)
chains

1 repeat of 3 chains

(1)
chain

(1)
chain

(1)
chain

Start of edging

(44)
stitches

First row of edging
Single crochet for
picking up stitches

1 stitch
increase

Pick up
16 stitches

Pick up
44 stitches

1 stitch
increase

Pick up
16 stitches

1 stitch
increase

Covered button (make 2)

Strap (make 2)

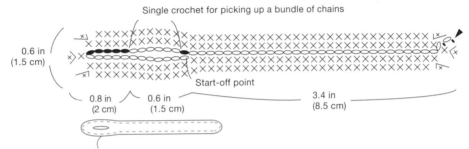

Single crochet for picking up a bundle of chains

0.6 in
(1.5 cm)

Start-off point

0.8 in
(2 cm)

0.6 in
(1.5 cm)

3.4 in
(8.5 cm)

Running stitches using double orange thread for the edge of the strap

Finish

1.6 in
(4 cm)

0.6 in
(1.5 cm)

Sew the covered buttons

Sew the straps

0.4 in (1 cm)

0.6 in (1.5 cm)

Sew roughly 0.6 in (1.5 cm)

6.6 in
(16.5 cm)
35 rows

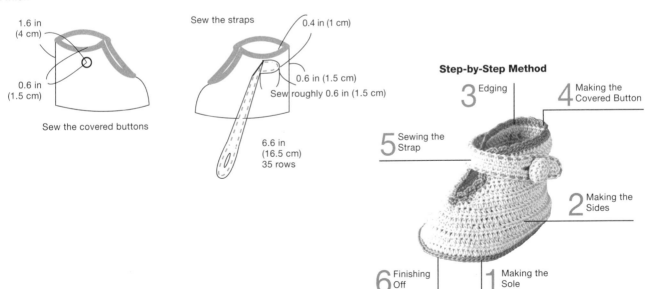

Step-by-Step Method

3 Edging

4 Making the
Covered Button

5 Sewing the
Strap

2 Making the
Sides

6 Finishing
Off

1 Making the
Sole

● MULTIPURPOSE COVER

See page 11 for photo; see Lacy Crochet Techniques (page 33) for stitch guide and illustrated instructions.

· · · · · · · · · · · · · · · · · · · ·

Materials

Green, 0.7 oz (2 0g)
Ivory, 0.5 oz (15 g)
Light brown, 0.5 oz (15 g)

Crochet hook
Size 4 (2 mm)

Pattern Size
10.2 in × 15.2 in (26 cm × 38.5 cm)

Crochet Steps

1 Making the Foundation
Cast-on and make 79 chains using the light brown thread.

2 Sewing the Base
Continuing from the cast-on stitch, make three foundation chains and work one row in double crochet as indicated on the diagram on the facing page. 2nd row: Make one foundation chain and repeat across one single crochet, three chains, one two-double crochet cluster and three chains. 3rd row: Make three foundation chains and repeat across two chains, one single crochet, two chains and one double crochet. Using the color table, repeat the pattern of the first three rows to stitch a total of 61 rows. Then, cut the thread.

3 Edging
Tie the green thread to the 61st row in the base and make one foundation chain. Work in single crochet around. 2nd row: Work chain, two double crochet clusters and picot pattern, as indicated on the diagram (see also Two Double Crochet Cluster and Chain Picot, on page 39).

Tip
It is easier to change threads when working the last stitch of the previous row.

Step-by-Step Method

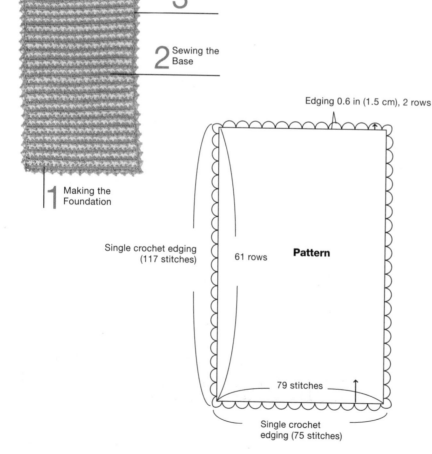

3 Edging

2 Sewing the Base

1 Making the Foundation

Edging 0.6 in (1.5 cm), 2 rows

Single crochet edging (117 stitches)

61 rows **Pattern**

79 stitches

Single crochet edging (75 stitches)

● Color Table for the Base

Row	Thread Color	
60th–61st Rows	Light brown	
59th Row	Ivory	
57th–58th Rows	Green	
56th Row	Ivory	
12th–13th Rows	Light brown	
11th Row	Ivory	
9th–10th Rows	Green	
8th Row	Ivory	
6th–7th Rows	Light brown	Repeat 10 times
5th Row	Ivory	
3rd–4th Rows	Green	
2nd Row	Ivory	
1st Row	Light brown	

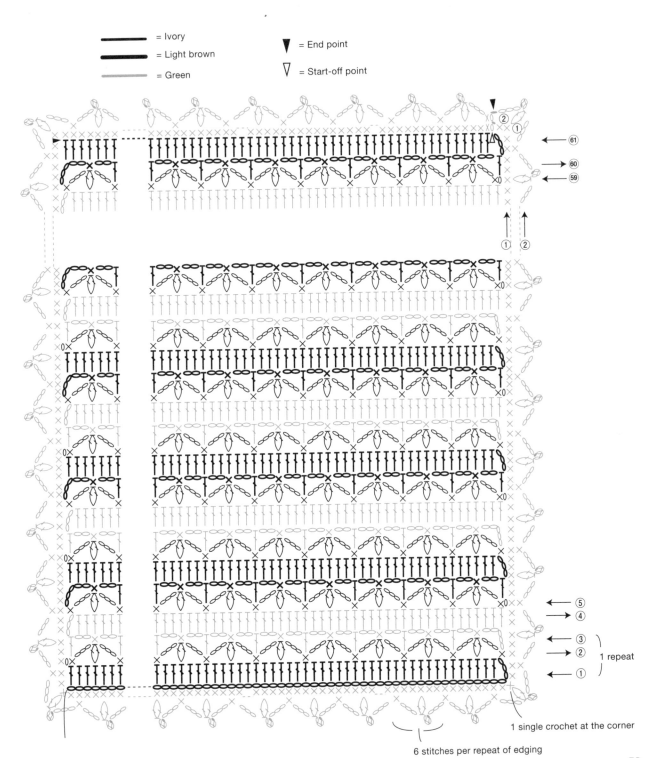

= Ivory

= Light brown

= Green

▼ = End point

▽ = Start-off point

② ①

← 61

→ 60

← 59

① ②

← 5

→ 4

← 3

→ 2

← 1

1 repeat

1 single crochet at the corner

6 stitches per repeat of edging

● LACE BASKET

See page 13 for photo; see Lacy Crochet Techniques (page 33) for stitch guide and illustrated instructions.

• • • • • • • • • • • • • • • • • •

Materials

Yellow, 0.7 oz (20 g)
4 wooden beads, 0.01 in (7 mm)

Crochet hook
Size 4 (2 mm)

Pattern Size

Bottom: 5.5 in (14 cm) diameter
Height: 1 in (2.5 cm)

Crochet Steps

1 Making the Foundation
Make a cast-on ring and one foundation chain. Do 8 single crochets into the ring.

3 Crocheting the Side Piece
Continuing from the base, make three foundation chains. 1st row: Pick up the back loop of the 12th row of the bottom side and work double crochet and chain pattern across. 2nd to 4th rows: Stitch through the net pattern as indicated on the diagram below. 5th row: Work across in reverse single crochet and chain. Draw through the foundation stitch.

2 Sewing the Bottom Side
Work 12 rows in double crochet, increasing in a circular pattern as indicated on the diagram on the facing page (see Two Double Crochet Increase, on page 38). The front side of the pattern will be the visible base of the basket.

4 Making the Handles
Leave about 8 inches (20 cm) of the thread's end, then make 25 chains. Single crochet the 1st row. To do the 2nd row, insert the hook into every other cast-on chain and do a single crochet. Weave into the 1st row, and leave about 8 inches (20 cm) of the thread at the end. Repeat to make the second handle.

5 Finishing Off
Sew a handle to the 3rd row of the side with the thread ends, then sew the beads on top. Repeat to attach the other handle.

Step-by-Step Method

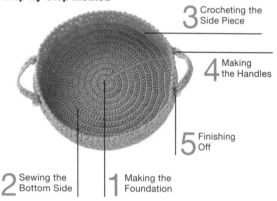

3 Crocheting the Side Piece

4 Making the Handles

5 Finishing Off

2 Sewing the Bottom Side

1 Making the Foundation

● Stitches and Increases for the Base

Row	Stitches	Increase
12th Row	160 Stitches	(+16 stitches)
11th Row	144 Stitches	(+16 stitches)
10th Row	128 Stitches	(+16 stitches)
9th Row	112 Stitches	(+16 stitches)
8th Row	96 Stitches	(+16 stitches)
7th Row	80 Stitches	(+8 stitches)
6th Row	72 Stitches	(+8 stitches)
5th Row	64 Stitches	(+16 stitches)
4th Row	48 Stitches	(+16 stitches)
3rd Row	32 Stitches	(+16 stitches)
2nd Row	16 Stitches	(+8 stitches)
1st Row	8 Stitches	

Handles (make 2)

② →
① ←

✕ = Weave through the cast-on chains

Finish

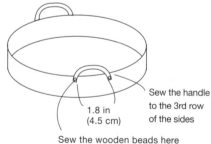

1.8 in (4.5 cm)

Sew the handle to the 3rd row of the sides

Sew the wooden beads here

Sides

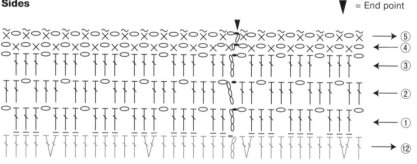

▼ = End point

⑤
④
③
②
①
⑫

Pick up the back loop of the double crochet in the previous row and purl.

Bottom

● SCISSORS CASE

See page 14 for photo; see Lacy Crochet Techniques (page 33) for stitch guide and illustrated instructions.

Materials

Light brown, 0.2 oz (5 g)
Felt backing, 5.5 in × 7.9 in
(14 cm × 20 cm)

Crochet hook
Size 6 (1.8 mm)

Darning needle

Pattern Size

4.7 in x 3 in (12 cm × 7 cm)

Crochet Steps

1 **Crocheting the Motif**
Make a cast-on ring and three foundation chains. Work double crochets and chains to make the cluster motif, as indicated on the diagrams. 2nd to 4th rows: Work single crochet net and expand the stitched work to a triangle shape. Stitch picots in the 5th row. Draw through the foundation chain to finish.

2 **Preparing the Felt Backing**
Cut the felt cloth according to the front and back shapes pictured and make holes as indicated with a sewing awl.

3 **Edging**
Attach the thread to the top of the felt piece and stitch the edging as indicated. Repeat to stitch the second edging on the other piece. Place the reverse sides of the felt backings together. Darn the edges.

4 **Finishing Off**
Sew the motif to the edge of the felt's upper side, weaving a single crochet stitch through the edging stitches.

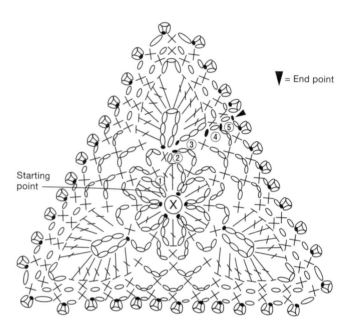

▼ = End point

Starting point

Step-by-Step Method

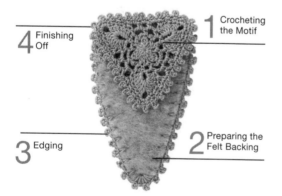

4 Finishing Off

3 Edging

1 Crocheting the Motif

2 Preparing the Felt Backing

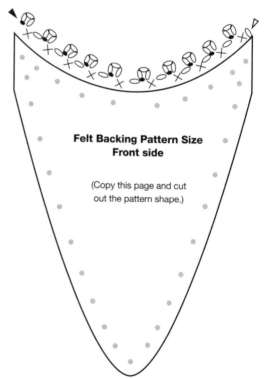

Felt Backing Pattern Size
Front side

(Copy this page and cut out the pattern shape.)

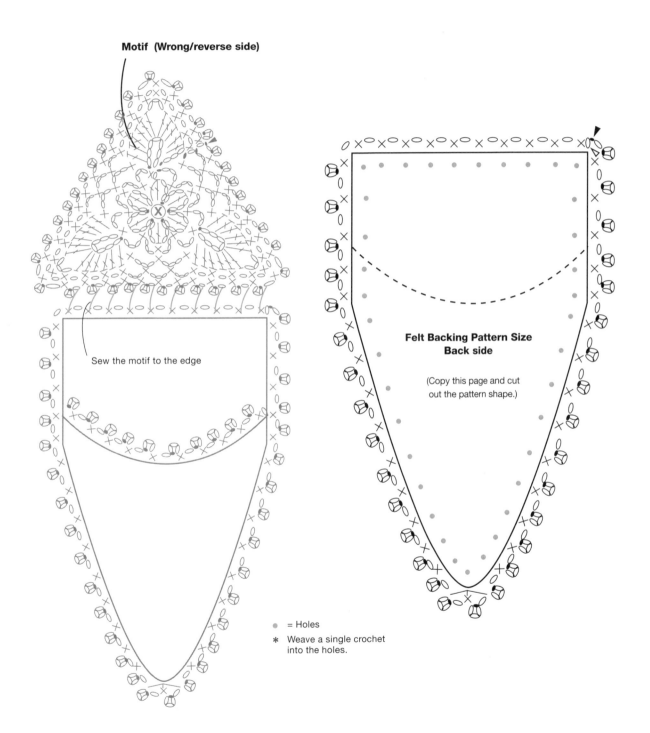

Motif (Wrong/reverse side)

Sew the motif to the edge

Felt Backing Pattern Size
Back side

(Copy this page and cut
out the pattern shape.)

● = Holes

＊ Weave a single crochet
into the holes.

● HOOK CASE

See page 15 for photo: see Lacy Crochet Techniques (page 33) for stitch guide and illustrated instructions.

. . . .

Materials

Lace thread
Orange, 1.1 oz (30 g)
Fabric liner, 10 in square (25.5 cm square); purchase a precut fabric square or hemstitch a piece of fabric by hand or using a sewing machine
2 beads, 0.4 (1 cm) in diameter

Crochet hook
Size 6 (1.8 mm)

Pattern Size

6.3 in × 10.8 in (16 cm × 27.5 cm)

Crochet Steps

1 Making the Foundation
Cast-on and make 81 chains.

2 Crocheting the Base
Make three foundation chains continuing from the cast-on chains, and work a flat crochet for 17 rows in chain and double crochet pattern, as indicated on the diagram on the facing page (see Flat Crocheting, on page 34).

3 Edging
Single crochet around, continuing from the base. 2nd row: Work chains and single crochets. 3rd row: Pick up a bundle of chains in the previous row and work single crochet pattern (see page 36).

4 Sewing the Laces
Double the thread and make 250 chains. Attach the beads to each end and knot the thread.

5 Making the Inner Pocket
Fold the liner as shown in the figure, and preferably sew by machine. (If hand stitching, use tight, even stitches and make double seams.)

6 Finishing Off
Pass the laces in the center through the left side of the base (8th row and 10th row), then sew. Place the inner pocket on the reverse side of the base and whipstitch together, preferably using a sewing machine.

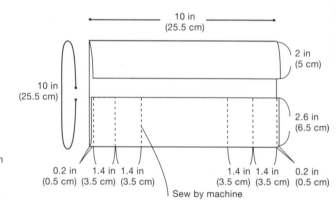

0.4 in (1 cm)
Edging
3 rows

**Felt Backing Pattern Size
Front side**

Single crochet the edges (51 stitches)

5.5 in (14 cm)
17 rows

10 in (25.5 cm)
81 stitches

Single crochet the edges (84 stitches)

Inner pocket

10 in (25.5 cm)

10 in (25.5 cm)

2 in (5 cm)

2.6 in (6.5 cm)

0.2 in (0.5 cm) · 1.4 in (3.5 cm) · 1.4 in (3.5 cm) · 1.4 in (3.5 cm) · 1.4 in (3.5 cm) · 0.2 in (0.5 cm)

Sew by machine

Step-by-Step Method

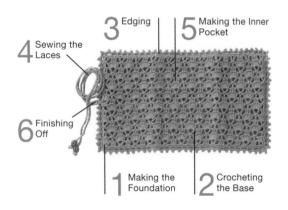

4 Sewing the Laces
3 Edging
5 Making the Inner Pocket
6 Finishing Off
1 Making the Foundation
2 Crocheting the Base

Finish

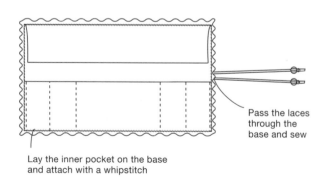

Lay the inner pocket on the base and attach with a whipstitch

Pass the laces through the base and sew

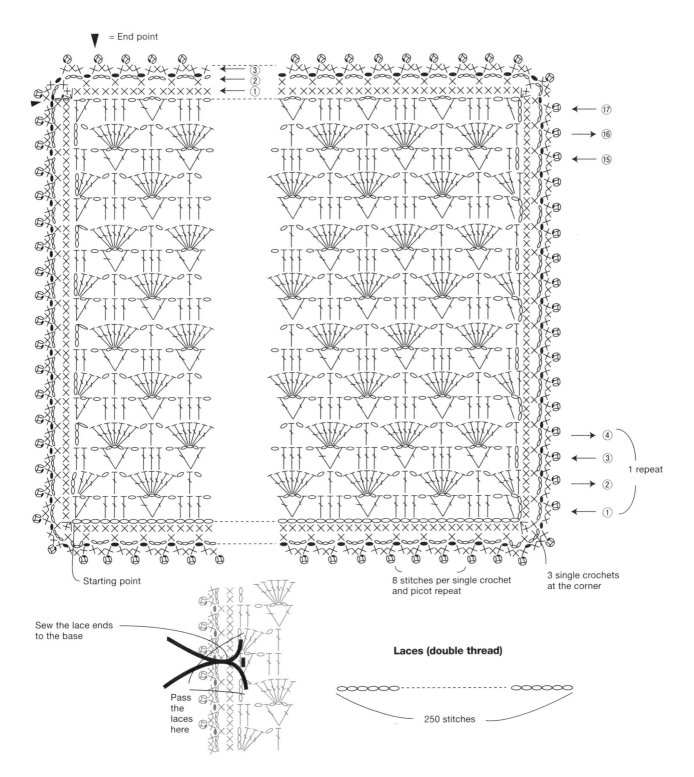

▼ = End point

③
②
①

→ ⑰
→ ⑯
← ⑮

④
③
②
①

1 repeat

Starting point

8 stitches per single crochet
and picot repeat

3 single crochets
at the corner

Sew the lace ends
to the base

Pass
the
laces
here

Laces (double thread)

250 stitches

● CORSAGE 1 (GERBERA)

See page 19 for photo; see Lacy Crochet Techniques (page 33) for stitch guide and illustrated instructions.

· · · · · · · · · · · · · · · · · · · ·

Materials

Lace thread
Ivory, 0.4 oz (10 g)
Light blue, 0.2 oz (5 g)
9 wooden beads, 0.2 in (0.5 cm) diameter
1 piece plastic padding, 0.9 in (2.4 cm) diameter
1 brooch pin, 1 in (2.5 cm) wide

Crochet hook
Size 6 (1.8 mm)

Pattern Size

Approx. 3.4 in (9.0 cm) square

Crochet Steps

1 **Making the Base and Petals**
Make a cast-on ring and one foundation chain, then do single crochets into the ring. 2nd to 4th rounds: Work three rounds in single crochet, increasing 6 stitches on the 2nd round and 6 in the 3rd round, end with 18 stitches in the 4th round. 5th row (petals): Stitch one single crochet and 15 chains to form the foundation of each petal. Stitch three foundation chains, 13 double crochets, 1 half double crochet, and 1 single crochet on the chains. Make one single crochet next to the 3rd row. Repeat to make a total of 18 petals. Single crochet around the petals using light blue thread.

2 **Sewing the Flower Motif**
Make a cast-on ring and three foundation chains, then do 17 double crochets in the ring. 2nd row: Make one foundation chain and single crochet around for a total of 18 stitches.

3 **Finishing Off**
Place the plastic padding in the center of the flower, put the motif on top, then whipstitch them together. Steam iron to adjust the shape. Sew the brooch pin on the reverse side and beads along the edge of the flower motif.

Petals and Base

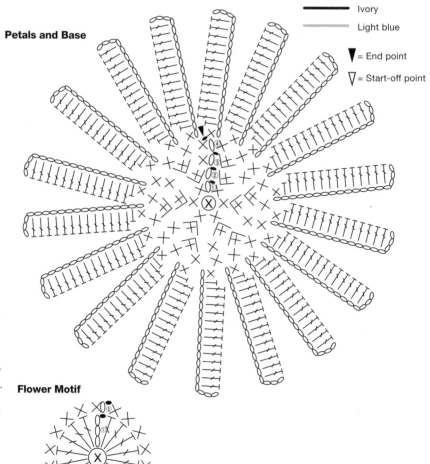

Ivory
Light blue
▼ = End point
▽ = Start-off point

Flower Motif

1.0 in
(2.5 cm)

Step-by-Step Method

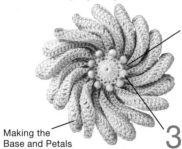

1 Making the Base and Petals

2 Sewing the Flower Motif

3 Finishing Off

Finish

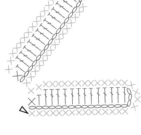

Wooden beads
Flower motif
Plastic padding
Base
Brooch pin

Sew the flower motif, arranging the petals so they overlap

Edge of Petals

● CORSAGE 2 (ROSE)

See page 19 for photo; see Lacy Crochet Techniques (page 33) for stitch guide and illustrated instructions.

Materials

Lace thread
Brown, 0.4 oz (10 g)
Light brown, 0.2 oz (6 g)
12 wooden beads, 0.2 in (0.5 cm)
1 brooch pin, 1 in (2.5 cm) wide

Crochet hook
Size 6 (1.8 mm)

Pattern Size

Approx. 3.4 in square (8.5 cm square)

Crochet Steps

1 Crocheting the Small Petals
Make eight chains and draw through the first chain to make a ring. Pick up a bundle of the ring to work the first row as indicated on the diagram: Stitch the 2nd row (petal shapes) into the previous row's stitches. Make two petals—one in each color.

2 Crocheting the Large Petals
Stitch the large petals using the same method as used for the small petals, adding an additional round as indicated on the diagram.

3 Making the Leaves
Make one leaf in each color. Make 13 chains. Make one foundation chain, then work the single crochet, half double crochet, and double crochet pattern into 6 chains as indicated on the diagram. Slip stitch to cross the chains, then stitch the pattern to make the sides appear symmetrical. Work a 3-chain picot on the edge, and backtrack the leaf's center with 6 slip stitches. Make 3 slip stitches to backtrack. Make 10 chains and start the next leaf. From the second leaf, add a slip stitch in the middle of the leaf pattern so that the leaves are connected.

4 Making the Flower Foundation
Make a cast-on ring and one foundation chain. Do 6 single crochets and work 7 rows, increasing 6 stitches for each row as indicated on the diagram on page 68.

5 Finishing Off
Arrange the small and large petals together in an overlapped shape, and sew 3 wooden beads in the center so that the figure looks like a rose. Sew 2 leaves and 4 roses to the base, and the brooch pin on the reverse side.

Small Petals

(Make 2 with light brown and brown threads)

Large Petals

(Make 2 petals with light brown and brown threads)

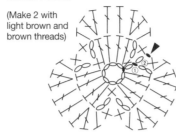

Leaves

(Make with light brown and brown threads)

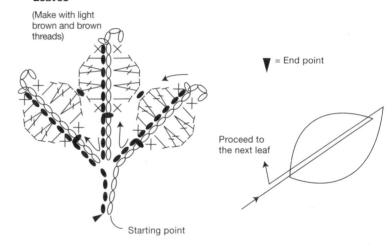

▼ = End point

Proceed to the next leaf

Starting point

Step-by-Step Method

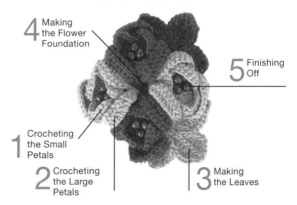

4 Making the Flower Foundation

5 Finishing Off

1 Crocheting the Small Petals

2 Crocheting the Large Petals

3 Making the Leaves

Finished petals

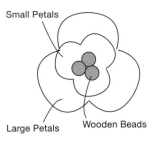

Small Petals

Large Petals — Wooden Beads

● Stitches and Increases for Foundation

Row	Stitches	Increase
7th Row	42 Stitches	+ 6 stitches
6th Row	36 Stitches	+ 6 stitches
5th Row	30 Stitches	+ 6 stitches
4th Row	24 Stitches	+ 6 stitches
3rd Row	18 Stitches	+ 6 stitches
2nd Row	12 Stitches	+ 6 stitches
1st Row	6 Stitches	

Flower Foundation (1 brown piece)

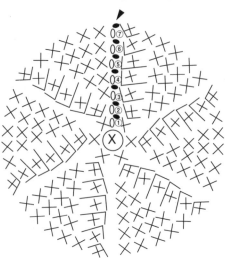

● COIN PURSE

See page 21 for photo; see Lacy Crochet Techniques (page 33) for stitch guide and illustrated instructions.

Materials

Lace thread
Orange, 0.4 oz (10 g)
Light blue, 0.1 oz (2 g)
1 Purse metal frame: 26 holes, W 3 in x H 1.6 in
(W 7.5 cm x H 4 cm)

Crochet hook
Size 6 (1.75 mm)

Darning needle

Pattern Size

4 in × 2.4 in (10 cm × 6 cm), excluding purse frame

Crochet Steps

1 Making the Foundation
Make a cast-on ring and one foundation chain, then do 6 single crochets into the ring.

4 Finishing Off
Sew the base to the purse frame (close the four stitches that were skipped), as indicated in the diagram on the facing page.

2 Crocheting the Base
Work the next 13 rounds in single crochet, as indicated on the diagram on the facing page. 15th to 25th rows: Work rounds evenly, 84 stitches per round without increasing.

3 Making the Leaf Motif
Make 7 chains. Make one foundation chain, then work single crochet, half double crochet, and double crochet pattern (as indicated in the diagram on the facing page) into 7 chains. Make 3 chains and a slip stitch. Then, work the other side of the 7 chains in the same way. Make a slip stitch on the foundation chain. Make 5 chains and sew them to the purse frame using a single crochet. Make 12 chains and repeat the motif pattern. Make one slip stitch and work on the other side of the chains in the same way. Make 3 chains, 1 slip stitch, then cut the thread.

Step-by-Step Method

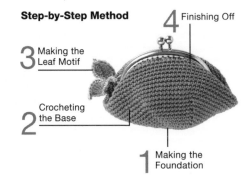

3 Making the Leaf Motif

2 Crocheting the Base

4 Finishing Off

1 Making the Foundation

Base

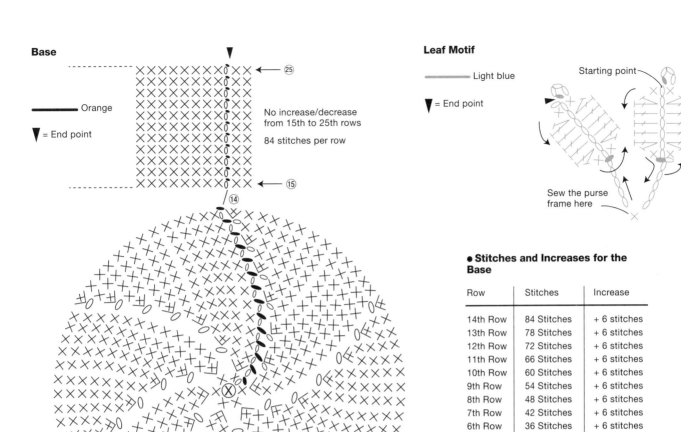

—— Orange

▼ = End point

No increase/decrease from 15th to 25th rows

84 stitches per row

Leaf Motif

—— Light blue

▼ = End point

Starting point

Sew the purse frame here

● **Stitches and Increases for the Base**

Row	Stitches	Increase
14th Row	84 Stitches	+ 6 stitches
13th Row	78 Stitches	+ 6 stitches
12th Row	72 Stitches	+ 6 stitches
11th Row	66 Stitches	+ 6 stitches
10th Row	60 Stitches	+ 6 stitches
9th Row	54 Stitches	+ 6 stitches
8th Row	48 Stitches	+ 6 stitches
7th Row	42 Stitches	+ 6 stitches
6th Row	36 Stitches	+ 6 stitches
5th Row	30 Stitches	+ 6 stitches
4th Row	24 Stitches	+ 6 stitches
3rd Row	18 Stitches	+ 6 stitches
2nd Row	12 Stitches	+ 6 stitches
1st Row	6 Stitches	

● **How to Sew the Purse Frame**

Skip some stitches as shown in the figure below to sew 31 stitches into 26 holes.

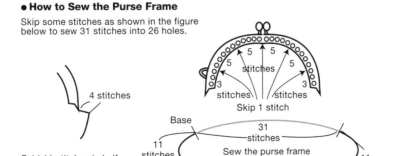

4 stitches

Fold 11 stitches in half, roll 4 stitches, and sew with overcast stitches

5 stitches
5 stitches
Skip 1 stitch
3 stitches
3 stitches

Base
31 stitches
11 stitches
Sew the purse frame
31 stitches
11 stitches

● MOBILE PHONE CASE

See page 18 for photo; see Lacy Crochet Techniques (page 33) for stitch guide and illustrated instructions.

Materials

Lace thread
Light blue, 0.9 oz (26 g)
1 snap, hook and D-ring, 0.6 in (1.5 cm) wide

Crochet hook
Size 6 (1.8 mm)

Pattern Size

3.7 in × 3 in (9.5 cm × 7.5 cm); gusset 1.2 in (3 cm), excluding the handle

Finish

Crochet Steps

1 Making the Foundation
Cast-on and make 25 chains.

2 Crocheting the Upper Side of the Base
Make one foundation chain continuing from the cast-on stitch, then repeat one single crochet and five double crochets across for a total of 21 rows, as indicated on the diagram on the facing page. Work a reverse single crochet on the 22nd row.

3 Crocheting the Lower Side of the Base
Stitch the other side of the cast-on chains in the same way as in step 2 to form the lower side of the base. Work a reverse single crochet on the 21st row.

4 Sewing Gusset A and B
Continue from the base to make the gussets. Gusset A: Make three foundation chains on the points indicated in the diagram, then work in double crochet for nine stitches. Repeat a single crochet and a double crochet row alternately, and decrease the stitches by a 2-double crochet decrease at both ends of the 17th and 19th rows. Gusset B: Work in the same way as Gusset A but continue for a total of 45 rows.

5 Finishing Off
Darn the base and gusset with single crochet stitches. When the darning is completed, work a single crochet row at the top of the gusset using the same thread. Loop through the D-ring with the tip of gusset A and through the snap hook with the tip of gusset B and darn. Then work a single crochet on the other side of the gussets through the base.

Step-by-Step Method

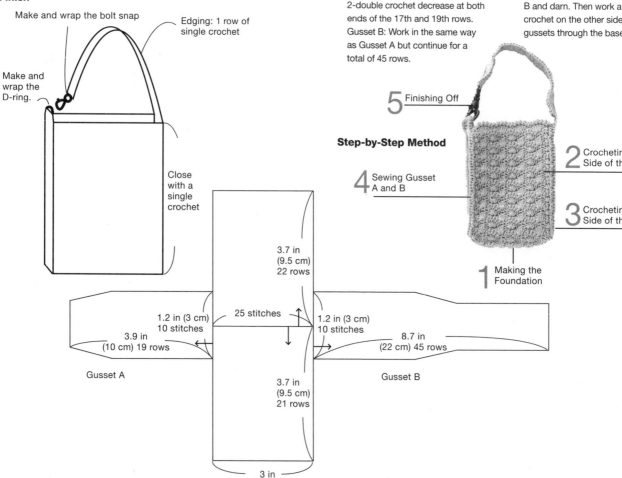

Make and wrap the bolt snap

Make and wrap the D-ring.

Edging: 1 row of single crochet

Close with a single crochet

5 Finishing Off

4 Sewing Gusset A and B

2 Crocheting the Upper Side of the Base

3 Crocheting the Lower Side of the Base

1 Making the Foundation

3.7 in (9.5 cm) 22 rows

1.2 in (3 cm) 10 stitches

25 stitches

1.2 in (3 cm) 10 stitches

3.9 in (10 cm) 19 rows

8.7 in (22 cm) 45 rows

Gusset A

Gusset B

3.7 in (9.5 cm) 21 rows

3 in (7.5 cm)

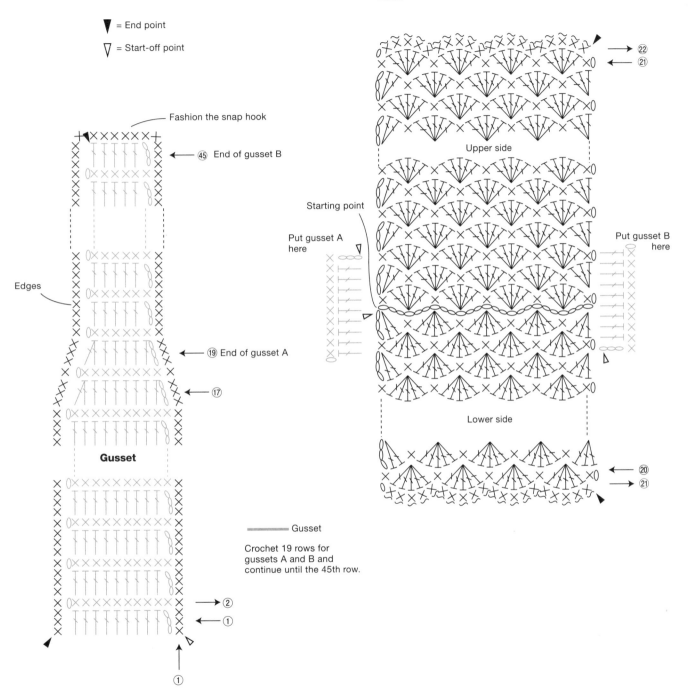

Base

▼ = End point

▽ = Start-off point

Fashion the snap hook

← ㊺ End of gusset B

Edges

← ⑲ End of gusset A

← ⑰

Gusset

→ ②

← ①

▽

① ↑

Upper side

Starting point

Put gusset A
here

Put gusset B
here

Lower side

→ ㉒
← ㉑

← ⑳
→ ㉑

Gusset

Crochet 19 rows for
gussets A and B and
continue until the 45th row.

● POTPOURRI SACHET 1 (FLOWERS)

See page 20 for photo; see Lacy Crochet Techniques (page 33) for stitch guide and illustrated instructions.

Materials

Lace thread
Ivory, 0.5 oz (15 g)
Yellow, 0.4 oz (10 g)
Grosgrain ribbon, 27.6 in x 0.2 in (70 cm x 0.6 cm)

Crochet hook
Size 6 (1.8 mm)

Pattern Size

Approx. 4.7 in square (12 cm square), excluding the handles

Crochet Steps

1 Crocheting the Sides
Make a cast-on ring and one foundation chain, then do six single crochets into the ring. 2nd row: Work in single crochets increasing by six stitches for a total of 12 stitches. 3rd row: Change thread color and make three foundation chains. Then, work a 3-double crochet decrease. Repeat five double chains and a 4-double crochet decrease around, then draw through the first foundation chain. Cut off the thread. Make six more motifs in the same way, attaching them to the first motif as directed below. Work single crochets, chains, and double crochets to form the outer rounds. Then, make a second side piece.

2 Making the Gusset
Make 87 chains and three foundation chains. Repeat one chain and one double crochet across.

3 Attaching the Gusset and Edging
Tie the thread at the point indicated on the diagram on the facing page and work a single crochet to stitch the motifs to the gusset. Single crochet all around including the section where the gusset does not show. Then, crochet over the edges of the gusset. Change the thread and stitch one more row. Work on the back of the sachet the same way.

4 Finishing Off
Pass the ribbon through the gusset as indicated on the diagram below and tie.

Gusset

9 in (23 cm)
87 stitches

Pass the ribbon through every stitch

Step-by-Step Method

4 Finishing Off

3 Attaching the Gusset and Edging

2 Making the Gusset

1 Crocheting the Sides

● How to Connect the Motifs

1 Complete one piece, then connect it at the center of the five chains in the outer row of the second piece.

2 Make two chains in the second piece, then insert the hook into the third chain of the first piece and draw through.

3 The pieces are now connected. Continue stitching the remaining part of the first piece.

4 Connect the third piece at the outer row with the first two pieces.

Sides (make 2)

Start stitching the gusset here
(Chart is enlarged)

Starting point for the last row

End the gusset stitch here

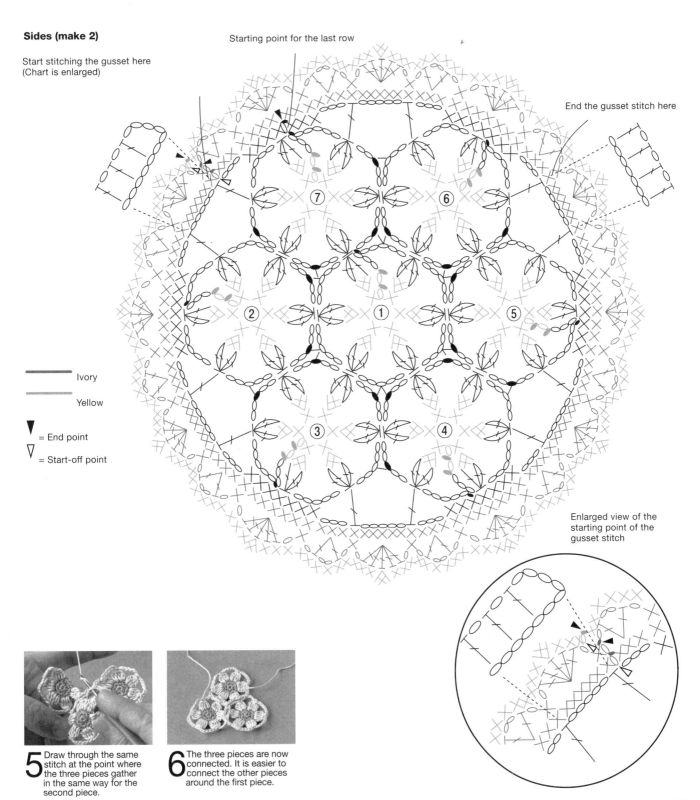

Ivory

Yellow

▼ = End point

▽ = Start-off point

Enlarged view of the
starting point of the
gusset stitch

5 Draw through the same
stitch at the point where
the three pieces gather
in the same way for the
second piece.

6 The three pieces are now
connected. It is easier to
connect the other pieces
around the first piece.

● POTPOURRI SACHET 2 (LEAVES)

See page 20 for photo; see Lacy Crochet Techniques (page 33) for stitch guide and illustrated instructions.

Materials

Lace thread
Ivory, 0.5 oz (15 g)
Green, 0.4 oz (10 g)
57 small ball beads (yellow green)
54 small ball beads (transparent yellow green)
Some wire

Crochet hook
Size 6 (1.8 mm)

Darning needle

Pattern Size

Approx. 4.7 in square (12 cm square), excluding the handles

Crochet Steps

1 Making the Foundation
Cast-on and make 34 chains.

2 Crocheting the Base Pieces
Make three foundation chains continuing from the cast-on stitch, then pick up the back loop of the chains to work a flat crochet for 14 rows, in the double crochet and a single crochet pattern as indicated in the diagram on the facing page. Make another piece of the same pattern.

3 Sewing the Sequence of Edges and Handles
Put the reverse sides of the two base sections together, and close the sides and bottom with a single crochet. To form the mouth section, work a single crochet stitching on each side without the sections together, and continue to stitch the handles. See How to Make the Mouth and Handles on the facing page.

4 Making the Leaf Motifs
Knit 16 leaves, attaching them together, for the border decoration. Make one more leaf for the center. See How to Make the Green Leaves.

5 Decorating with Beads
Pass the wire through the beads and shape the pattern into a leaf as indicated on the diagram.

6 Finishing Off
Sew the leaf sequence motif at the front edge of the main piece, then attach the leaf motif and the beaded decoration to the center.

Beaded Decoration

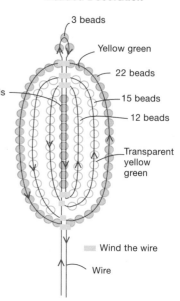

3 beads
Yellow green
22 beads
15 beads
12 beads
10 beads
Transparent yellow green

▨ Wind the wire

Wire

Step-by-Step Method

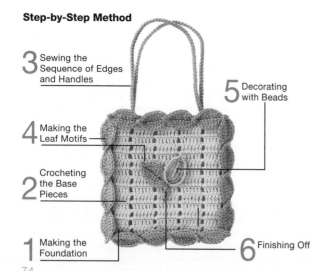

3 Sewing the Sequence of Edges and Handles

4 Making the Leaf Motifs

2 Crocheting the Base Pieces

1 Making the Foundation

5 Decorating with Beads

6 Finishing Off

Leaf Motif (green leaves)

Starting point

1 leaf

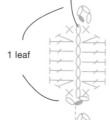
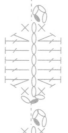

Center leaf

Starting point

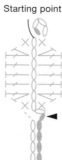

● How to Make the Green Leaves

1 Make seven chains.

2 Make one foundation chain, then stitch a single crochet, half double crochet, and double crochets into the seven chains.

3 Make three chains and a slip stitch into the first chain. Continue working the same pattern on the other side of the seven chains.

4 Do a slip stitch on the foundation chain as in step 2.

5 Repeat steps 1 to 4 to make 16 leaves.

● How to Make the Center Leaf

Steps 1 to 3 are the same steps as for sewing the green leaves. Continue, making five chains, then do a slip stitch on them. Draw through the foundation chain to finish the pattern.

● How to Make the Mouth and Handles

1 Work in single crochet for 28 stitches on the front part of the mouth, then continue making 70 chains.

2 Draw through the 7th single crochet from the right edge of the base piece.

3 Work a slip stitch back across the 70 chains.

4 Work in single crochet on the remaining five stitches of the mouth, then continue working on the back side in the same way.

Edging
(70 stitches)

3.7 in
(9.5 cm)
14 rows

3.7 in
(9.5 cm)
34 stitches

Single crochet for edges
42 stitches

Single crochet for edges
34 stitches

70 slip stitches

—— Ivory

—— Green

▼ = End point

▽ = Start-off point

70 chains

Start of edges

5

4

1

2

3

→ ⑭

← ⑬

← ③

→ ②

← ①

Finish

Sew only the front part of the motif

Wind the wire for the beads around the border of the stem and leaves

1 stitch at the corner

Starting point

● DECORATIVE STRINGS 1 (BALLS)

See page 22 for photo; see Lacy Crochet Techniques (page 33) for stitch guide and illustrated instructions.

Materials

Lace thread
Green, 0.2 oz (5 g)
Light blue, 0.2 oz (5 g)
Yellow, 0.2 oz (5 g)
some cotton
8 buttons, 0.3 in (0.8 cm) diameter
2 buttons, 0.5 in (1.3 cm) diameter

Crochet hook
Size 6 (1.8 mm)

Pattern Size

22.1 in (56 cm) long

Crochet Steps

1 Making the Balls
Make a cast-on ring and one foundation chain, then do 8 single crochets into the ring. Work the increases to stretch the circular pattern, then a decrease round, as indicated on the diagram to the right. Place the cotton inside when the 6th row is complete. Then, pass the thread through the stitches in the last round and tighten. Cut off the thread, leaving about 2.4 inches. Make two balls of each color.

2 Making the String
Take three strands of thread (one of each color) and make 90 chains.

3 Decorating with Buttons
Pass the thread through the buttons and tie to make eight decorative buttons.

4 Finishing Off
Attach the balls and decorative buttons to the ends of the chains, then sew a button over the knot. Repeat for both ends.

Decorative Buttons

2 green buttons

2 buttons each of light blue and yellow

Approx. 2.4 in (6 cm)

Approx. 2.4 in (6 cm)

Button, 0.3 in (0.8 cm) diameter

Button, 0.3 in (0.8 cm) diameter

Pass the thread through the buttonhole and tie closely to the button

2 balls of each color

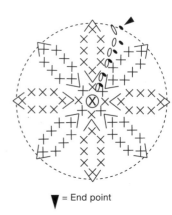

▼ = End point

3 strands of strings
1 string of each color

└── 90 stitches ──┘

Button, 0.5 in (1.3 cm) diameter

Tie the balls and decorative buttons with chain stitches, then sew them with the button.

Finish

Step-by-Step Method

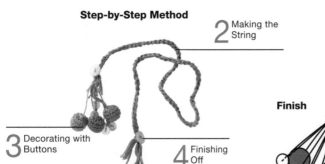

2 Making the String

3 Decorating with Buttons

4 Finishing Off

1 Making the Balls

● DECORATIVE STRINGS 2 (TASSELS)

See page 22 for photo; see Lacy Crochet Techniques (page 33) for stitch guide and illustrated instructions.

Materials

Lace thread
Orange, 0.2 oz (5 g)
Green, 0.2 oz (5 g)
Light blue, 0.2 oz (5 g)
Yellow, 0.2 oz (5 g)
Brown, 0.2 oz (5 g)
Light brown, 0.2 oz (5 g)
20 buttons, 0.5 in (1.2 cm) diameter (optionally in colors as indicated on the diagram)
14 buttons, 0.3 in (0.8 cm) diameter

Crochet hook
Size 6 (1.75 mm)

Pattern Size

42.1 in (107 cm) long

Crochet Steps

1 Making the Small Motifs
Make a cast-on ring and three foundation chains, leaving the thread's end longer, then do 11 double crochets into the ring. Draw through the foundation chain and make 20 chains.

2 Making the Large Motifs
Make a cast-on ring and four foundation chains, leaving the thread's end longer, then do 21 treble crochets into the ring. Draw through the foundation chain and make 12 chains. Do a slip stitch to connect it with the small motif

3 Finishing off
Repeat steps 1 and 2 to connect a total of 17 large and small motifs. Make 20 chains on the last small motif, then tie the tassels at both ends. Sew buttons to each side of the motif.

Step-by-Step Method

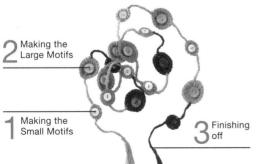

2 Making the Large Motifs

1 Making the Small Motifs

3 Finishing off

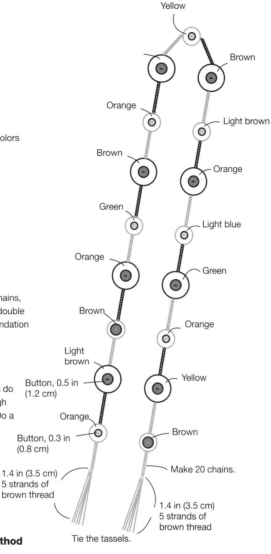

Yellow
Brown
Orange
Light brown
Brown
Orange
Green
Light blue
Orange
Green
Brown
Orange
Light brown
Yellow
Button, 0.5 in (1.2 cm)
Orange
Button, 0.3 in (0.8 cm)
Brown
Make 20 chains.

1.4 in (3.5 cm)
5 strands of brown thread

1.4 in (3.5 cm)
5 strands of brown thread

Tie the tassels.

How to Make the Tassels

Materials
5 strands of thread, 2.76 in (7 cm)
1 strand of long thread

Cut the thread into 2.8 inch (7 cm) lengths and gather them together. Tie the center and fold the bundle in half. Tie one end of the tie to the last chain of the decorative strings. Wind the other end of the tie around the neck of the tassel and tie it tightly.

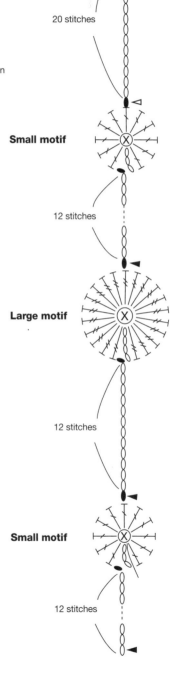

▼ = End point

▽ = Start-off point

20 stitches

Small motif

12 stitches

Large motif

12 stitches

Small motif

12 stitches

● MINI BAG 1 (PETALS)

See page 23 for photo; see Lacy Crochet Techniques (page 33) for stitch guide and illustrated instructions.

Materials

Lace thread
Light brown, 0.1 oz (4 g)
Brown, 0.1 oz (2 g)
Linen bag, H 7.1 in × W 5.9 in (H 18 cm × W 15 cm)
Sewing needle and thread

Crochet hook
Size 6 (1.8 mm)

Pattern Size

1 piece of flower motif, 1.6 in (4 cm) diameter

Crochet Steps

1 Making the Foundation
Make a cast-on ring and one foundation chain, then do 12 single crochets of into the ring.

2 Making the Petals
2nd row: Make one foundation chain and another foundation for the petals with one single crochet, five chains and a single crochet around, as indicated on the diagram. 3rd row: Pick up a bundle of chains in the previous row and work a single crochet, half double crochet, double crochet, and treble crochet pattern around. Repeat to make four more petals.

3 Finishing Off
Sew the motifs to the bag with a sewing thread.

Step-by-Step Method

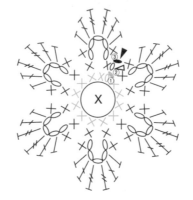

2 Making the Petals (make 5)

3 Finishing Off

1 Making the Foundation

— = Light brown
— = Brown
▼ = End point
▽ = Start-off point

● MINI BAG 2 (BUTTONS)

See page 23 for photo; see Lacy Crochet Techniques (page 33) for stitch guide and illustrated instructions.

Materials

Lace thread
Brown, 0.3 oz (8 g)
Orange, few strands
Yellow, few strands

Buttons
3 pieces, 0.3 in (0.8 cm)
1 piece, 0.4 in (1 cm)
4 pieces, 0.5 in (1.3 cm)
2 pieces, 0.6 in (1.5 cm)
1 piece, 0.7 in (1.8 cm)
1 piece, 0.9 in (2.3 cm)
Linen bag, H 7.1 in × W 5.9 in (L 18 cm × W 15 cm)

Crochet hook
Size 4 (2 mm)

Crochet Steps

1 Making Cross-stitches
Lay the linen bag flat or use a sewing hoop to hold in place. Work in cross stitch with a single strand thread as shown in the diagram below.

2 Sewing the Buttons
Sew the buttons as indicated on the diagram. Use four strands of thread to tie decorative ties on the buttons. Sew on the remaining buttons in a cross pattern.

3 Attaching the Fringe
Sew on the fringe as shown on the facing page.

Step-by-Step Method

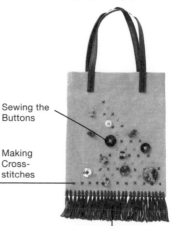

2 Sewing the Buttons

1 Making Cross-stitches

3 Attaching the Fringe

How to Attach the Fringe

Materials

3 strands of thread in 27 bundles,
4.7 in (12 cm)
Sewing awl
Glue

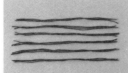

1 Prepare 27 bundles, three strands of thread each.

2 Make holes with a sewing awl, 0.3 inch (0.8 cm) from the bottom edge of the bag, leaving a 0.2 inch (0.5 cm) distance between the holes.

3 Insert the hook from the back and pull a triplet of thread through the holes.

4 Pass the thread's end through the ring that is pulled out, then fasten it.

5 Cut the ends to the same length. Strengthen the knot with a little glue.

● Button and Thread Sizes

Button No.	Size (in/cm)	Thread Color	Mode
1	0.3/0.8	Orange	Tie
2	0.4/1.0	Yellow	Sew
3	0.3/0.8	Brown	Tie
4	0.3/0.8	Brown	Tie
5	0.7/1.8	Orange	Sew
6	0.6/1.5	Yellow	Sew
7	0.5/1.3	Yellow	Tie
8	0.5/1.3	Orange	Tie
9	0.6/1.5	Brown	Tie
10	0.9/2.3	Orange	Tie
11	0.5/1.3	Brown	Sew
12	0.5/1.3	Yellow	Tie

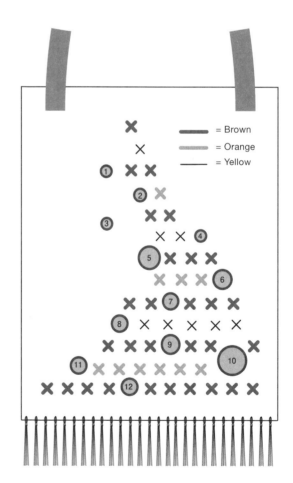

Design Credits

Coasters design and crochet: SACHIYO*FUKAO • Pot Holders design and crochet: SACHIYO*FUKAO; hooks by AWABEES • Tissue Box Cover design and crochet: SACHIYO*FUKAO • Jar Covers design and crochet: SACHIYO*FUKAO • Baby Shoes design and crochet: Yasuko Sebata; stuffed animal and cards by AWABEES • Doily 1 Round design and crochet: Mayumi Kawai • Doily 2 Square design: Mayumi Kawai; crochet: Itsuko Yoshioka; bottle by AWABEES • Multipurpose Cover design: Mayumi Kawai; crochet: Itsuko Yoshioka • Pincushion design and crochet: SACHIYO*FUKAO • Lace Basket design and crochet: SACHIYO*FUKAO; lace needle, bottle, beads, and pins by Au Temps Jadis • Scissors Case design and crochet: Mayumi Kawai • Hook Case design and crochet: Mayumi Kawai • Braids 1 and 2 design: Mayumi Kawai; crochet: Sachiko Sekiya; cloth by Au Temps Jadis • Braid 3 design: Mayumi Kawai; crochet: Sachiko Sekiya; cloth and thread by Au Temps Jadis • Mobile Phone Case design and crochet: Yasuko Sebata • Corsages design and crochet: Yasuko Sebata • Potpourri Sachets design and crochet: Yasuko Sebata • Coin Purse design and crochet: Yasuko Sebata • Decorative Strings design and crochet: Mayumi Kawai • Mini Bags design and crochet: Mayumi Kawai.

About the Author

SHUFU-TO-SEIKATSU SHA
Established in 1935, SHUFU-TO-SEIKATSU SHA is a well-noted lifestyle magazine in Japan that publishes on various subjects: women, housewife, fashion, health, home living, and many others. Its trendy magazine, LEON, has gained extreme popularity for its new editorial style. SHUFU-TO-SEIKATSU SHA publishes approximately 500 titles annually.